The Dumb Runner Reader

The Dumb Runner Reader

Choice Bits & Tasty Morsels,
2015–2017

MARK REMY

Copyright © 2017 Mark Remy
markremy.com

All rights reserved. No part of this publication may be reproduced, distributed, or transmitted in any form or by any means, including photocopying, recording, or other electronic or mechanical methods, without the prior written permission of the publisher, except in the case of brief quotations embodied in critical reviews.

Laurelhurst Media
3439 NE Sandy Blvd, #7170
Portland, OR 97232

ISBN: 197654761X
ISBN-13: 978-1976547614

For Sarah

INTRODUCTION

In late 2015 I launched DumbRunner.com, "an online destination for runners who enjoy laughter and pie."

I could go on and on about why I chose to do so, and what exactly I hoped to accomplish with Dumb Runner, and so forth. But I won't. (You're welcome.) Instead, I'll just share this, from the site's ABOUT page:

Here is what you will find at Dumb Runner: Odd and amusing news, Monty Python references, beginner-friendly advice, and answers to your most pressing questions. Some of it will even be running related!

Here is what you will not find: Bullshit.

While Dumb Runner does not take itself seriously, it does take running seriously. Most of the time.

This has been the guiding principle of Dumb Runner literally from day one. Two years in, I'm reasonably happy with the results—a lot of satire, a smattering of practical advice, at least one shout-out to Pratt & Whitney Commercial Jet Engines.[1]

This book represents a sort of "greatest hits" of what I've published to date. By which I mean, "the things I like best," starting with a piece about my penis. I hope you enjoy it. The book, I mean.

Mark Remy, December 2017

---

[1] See "SPONSORED: 5 Ways to Bust Out of a Rut, Brought to You by Pratt & Whitney Commercial Jet Engines," page 210.

My Large Penis Makes Running a Real Challenge

November 10, 2015

You may have missed it, with all this talk of Starbucks cups[1] and whatnot, but last week *The New York Times* published a Q&A on its Well blog titled "Ask Well: Does Foot Size Affect Running?"

Short answer: No, not really. That's the longer answer, too, except the longer one goes on for 338 words.

As usual, though, the "lamestream media" misses the real story. The question isn't whether foot size affects running but whether *penis size* does.

Readers, I am here today to tell you that, yes, it does.

And not for the better, either. You might think that that a large penis could confer some advantages on a runner—say, at the finish line of a close race, when the difference between first and second place may be a matter of inches. Or on a trail run, where a lower center of gravity may help during tricky, technical descents.

Well, it might, in rare cases. More often than not, however, a large penis acts more like an anchor, holding you back from running greatness. It is an albatross around your neck. Except without feathers and stuff and except that it's not around your neck, exactly.

---

[1] Remember when people *didn't* argue about coffee cups? Me neither.

Here are just a few of the many ways that owners of large penises suffer when it comes to running:

- Finding shorts that fit is exceedingly difficult.
- Wearing tights is out of the question.
- Compared with runners who have average-sized penises, they must work harder to maintain the same pace, due to the extra weight.
- They endure taunts and jokes from running buddies who can't resist using the phrase "schlong run" around them at every opportunity.
- When they run fast, the mass of their large penis creates such inertia that it is harder to stop quickly if they need to.
- When going through security, e.g., at a large race or at the airport en route to an event, they are more likely to be pulled aside for humiliating searches and pat-downs in the "swimsuit area."
- Navigating a porta potty can be difficult.
- People stare.

How do I know so much about the downside of running with a large penis? Because I have one, that's why. And I am tired of living "in the shadows." Today that changes. Today I say to all of my fellow large-penis-having runners: Stop feeling embarrassed. Stop worrying so much about your large penis and what others might think of it when you're out for a run. Start feeling proud.

Today I say to my fellow male runners: Embrace your large penis!

Also, if you've found some running shorts that work well for you, please let me know. Because, damn, guys. My penis.

Guest Opinion: Expensive Running Shoes Are Good and You Should Go Buy Some

December 8, 2015

Editor's note: The following is a guest column and does not reflect the views of Dumb Runner.

By Jon Swift, President
National Association of Running Shoe Manufacturers

Like many of you, I've read about the recent survey[1] suggesting that expensive running shoes don't work any better than cheaper ones, and that runners actually seem to rate cheaper shoes more favorably than expensive models.

This so-called study was "based on 134,867 reviews of 391 running shoes from 24 brands," and claimed to find that "the higher the list price, the lower ratings the running shoes get."

Allow me to offer a rebuttal to these findings: They are wrong. Expensive running shoes are better. How could they not be? They cost more money than cheaper models.

Things that cost a lot of money are better than things that don't cost a lot of money. This is Econ 101, folks, not

---

[1] This was a real survey.

to mention just plain old common sense. Perhaps you've heard the little saying "You get what you pay for?"

Honestly, I can't even believe we're having this discussion.

Still need convincing? Consider the facts:

- Clinical trials show that expensive running shoes have more, and better, features than cheaper ones.
- Expensive shoes have up to 60% more technology and 75% more science than cheaper ones.
- Things that cost a lot of money are better than things that don't cost a lot of money. I know I said that earlier, but it bears repeating.
- Thousands of runners are known to have been injured while wearing cheaper shoes.

And since that other "study" used so many charts and graphs, here is one of my own:

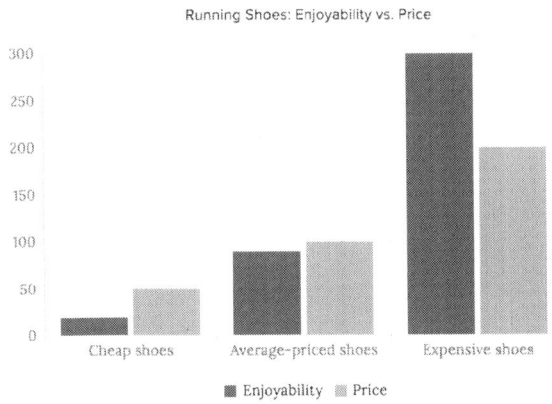

SOURCE: *National Association of Running Shoe Manufacturers*

I rest my case.

While we're at it, I understand that there are some ugly rumors floating around, claiming that running shoes may have a useful life beyond 350 to 500 miles, which everyone knows is how long running shoes last. This would be laughable if it weren't so alarming. Of course you need new running shoes every 350 to 500 miles. Because that is how long they last. Go look it up. It's common knowledge.

In fact, are your current running shoes new enough? Are you sure? Are you so sure you're willing to risk your health over it?

Take it from me, my friends: The moment your running shoes hit the 350-mile mark, you are in what we in the shoe biz call "The Danger Zone." And not the good, Kenny Loggins type, either. We're talking about the every-step-brings-you-closer-to-the-precipice type. Will running more than 350 to 500 miles in your shoes cause the muscles, tendons, and ligaments in your feet to seize up and rupture? Possibly mid-run? Throwing you off balance and sending you stumbling headlong into the path of a cement mixer whose driver will have to live out the rest of his days knowing that he's responsible for someone's death?

Will today's run be the one that ends in disaster?

Maybe. But, hey, you know what? Maybe not. Maybe that won't happen. Maybe you'll be fine, and you'll squeeze a few more miles out of your old, worn-out running shoes.

Your call.

In closing, let me just say that if you take nothing else away from this column, take this bit of advice, and I mean it from the bottom of my heart: Go buy expensive shoes.

If I Win the Powerball Jackpot, I Will Register for a Rock 'n' Roll Race

January 12, 2016

Like many people lately, I have lotto fever. How else to explain my dangerously high temperature, muscle and joint pain, and explosive diarrhea?

Also, how else to explain my obsession with this week's Powerball drawing? It's all I can think about. I know I'm not alone. I see the Facebook posts and news coverage. Seems like everyone has lotto fever. That's not surprising, considering how much money is up for grabs—as CNN Money reports, the jackpot "swelled to $1.5 billion on Tuesday morning." And it can only go up from there, thanks to all the hype. I predict the jackpot will continue swelling right up until Wednesday night's drawing, when it will groan and burst in a spectacular, blinding explosion of concentrated wealth, flattening everything in a 2-mile radius.

Will I win? Well, let's just say that with odds of 1 in 292 million, I like my chances.

Let's also say that I got a D in statistics, which, by the way, I pronounce without that first "t" sound, like this: "suh-TISS-tix."

Anyway.

Also like many people lately, I have thought a lot about

what I could do with my winnings. Which, for the record, would actually be about $930 million as a lump sum. I could buy an island! A McMansion! Heck, a mansion mansion! A Maserati for every day of the week!

Wait. No. I know exactly what I'll do when I win that $930 million.

I will register for a Rock 'n' Roll Marathon Series event.

Extravagant? Ostentatious? A vulgar display of obscene wealth? Perhaps. I don't care. Life is short.

And you know what? I won't even bother registering early. I'll wait till the last minute—when even signing up for the half will set me back 175 bucks.

Here's how it will go down:

I'll decide, on a whim, to run a half-marathon. I'll open my laptop, launch my browser, and type "runrocknroll.com." I'll choose the first available event, fill out the online registration form, enter my credit card info, then click REGISTER or whatever the little button says. I won't even give it a second thought. You know why?

Because I will be rich. Signing-up-for-a-Rock-'n'-Roll-event-on-a-whim rich. That's why.

Will I be annoyed by the mystery $14.99 "IT processing fee" that shows up during checkout?

Please. I will barely even notice it.

In fact, I will pay the $14.99 IT processing fee of the person behind me in line. That is the sort of rich person I will be.

Of course, I won't go crazy. You're always reading stories about ordinary people who win big jackpots and then wind up, a few years and dozens of Rock 'n' Roll races later, flat broke. So I will limit myself to just one or two RNR events per year. And I'll skip the merchandise options. Mostly.

This is my plan.

Don't worry, friends—I won't forget you when I'm swimming in cash and running multiple Rock 'n' Roll races per year with my other wealthy friends. I'll still see you at local, more affordable races, which I will make a point of attending, just to stay grounded and to ask whether anyone has change for a hundred. Underneath my Rock 'n' Roll Marathon Series technical tee, I'll be the same old Mark.

The rich are different from you and me, the saying goes. They have more RNR Marathon medals.

We shall see, friends. We shall see.

Quiz: Are You a Good Runner?

February 02, 2016

Dear reader, are you a good runner?

No, not good as in "fast and strong." I mean good as in "moral and ethical."

A recent article got me thinking about this. The article, on RunnersWorld.com, is titled "Badwater Application Asks Runners: Are You a Good Human Being?"

The article begins:

The Badwater ultramarathon, a 135-mile run from Death Valley to Mt. Whitney every July, is open for registration. Race organizers aren't just looking for any runners, though. ... They want athletes with a history of completing ultras. And they want good people to fill the 100-person field.

It then goes on to list a few of the questions Badwater applicants must answer. For instance:

What percentage of your athletic peers (not just your friends, but the wider circle of athletes who know you, or know of you) would say that YOU are a Good Human Being and Good Sportsman/woman?

Also:

Who is your Favorite Author and/or Your Favorite Book?

Admit it: Even just reading that, you're tempted to say, "Well, I guess my favorite author would have to be God, and my favorite book the Holy Bible," aren't you? Like some sort of phony baloney beauty pageant contestant or politician? You are. And you should be ashamed of yourself. That is precisely the sort of chicanery the organizers of Badwater do not need at their event. Good day to you, sir.

Or ma'am. Whichever.

While we're at it, you can also admit that as you read that you were judging whoever wrote those questions for their Use of Random Capitalization. Weren't you?

Jerk.

This particular event aside, though, I find this fascinating, for a few reasons.

1. It never occurred to me to gauge the goodness of runners. I suppose because, in my experience, the overwhelming majority of runners are very decent people. It sort of goes without saying.

2. Isn't talking about your own goodness a little... unseemly?

3. How effective can this approach be? Does anyone expect a horrible human being to get halfway through this application, see the "are you a Good Human Being" question, then walk away, saying, "Welp, that counts me out"? By definition, if you are a bad human being you won't think twice about lying about your badness.

4. Assuming you're even conscious of it. Which you probably aren't. Also in my experience, very few assholes know they're assholes. They think they're just fine.

Still, I appreciate what the Badwater folks are trying to do here. I just think that if they, or any event organizers, are looking to weed out Bad Human Beings, they could benefit from some sharper, more revealing questions.

If I were looking to separate the good runners from the bad, here's what I would ask:

When you finish an energy gel during a run, do you:

a. Tuck the empty package into a pocket until you reach a garbage can.

b. Drop it on the ground.

c. Stuff it down the throat of a baby bird that's fallen from its nest.

Do you believe that banditing a race is OK?

a. No, it's stealing.

b. Yes, if you start in the back and don't take water, a medal, etc.

c. Yes, and I grab as much free stuff as I can along the way, including banners and scaffolding. Because corporate greed.

Have you ever tried on shoes at a specialty running store, then gone home and ordered the same pair online?

a. No, that's awful. People do that?

b. Yes. Because corporate greed.

c. Oh, my God, that's brilliant. Why didn't I think of that before?

During your run a motorist rolls through a STOP sign, nearly hitting you before screeching to a halt. Do you:

a. Wave and smile at the motorist, who you can tell is startled and sheepish.

b. Shout and gesture angrily, possibly slapping the car's hood or trunk.

c. Fake an injury, sue the motorist, and, via court records, steal his identity so you can apply for multiple credit cards in his name, allowing you to try on dozens of pairs of shoes at specialty running stores before going home and using these bogus credit cards to order the shoes online.

As you enter the starting corral of a large race, do you:
a. Find the pace-per-mile sign that best reflects my current level of fitness.
b. Elbow your way toward the front of the field.
c. Elbow your way toward the front of the field—but not too far front, because then the race director could see that you don't have a bib number.

Have you ever published a satirical online article that irritated organizers of a well-known endurance event?
a. Gawrsh, no![1]
b. Yes.
c. I may have done it twice now.

If you answered mostly "A"s, you are a good runner. If you answered mostly "B"s, you are not.

Mostly "C"s? You are bad beyond redemption.

Jerk.

---

[1] A reference to my 2014 RunnersWorld.com column "Disney Acquires Badwater 135."

Running With Your Gun: FAQ

February 4, 2016

Readers, if you live in or around Upper Dublin or Abington township, Pennsylvania, do the authorities a favor and keep your eyes peeled for a lost handgun. Because one is missing.

Apparently an unnamed woman lost her gun during a run there last weekend, "in the Ardsley and North Hills sections," and dang if the police can find it. They've looked three times.[1]

An Upper Dublin police officer, who spoke to PhillyVoice.com, had this to say: "It appears the gun was

---

[1] Really.

misplaced."

Well, these things happen. Especially to newbies.

I assume that this woman is a newbie, because advanced runners know that you should always duct-tape your handgun to your palm before leaving the house. Hands get slick with sweat, especially during warm-weather runs, and holsters just aren't that reliable when you're bouncing up and down, as during a run or while waiting at an intersection for the WALK sign. Holsters are a poor idea for other reasons as well. (See following page.)

So we can't blame this woman, really. But we can endeavor to ensure that this sort of thing doesn't happen again. How? With education, that's how.

While we wait for the Pennsylvania woman's loaded gun to turn up—I'm sure someone of some age will find it and pick it up sooner or later—let's review some basics.

Q: Should I carry a firearm when I run?
A: Absolutely.

Why?
Why? Turn on the news! It's a dangerous world. Threats lurk everywhere. What if you're attacked by a "thug" on your run, or an ISIS? Or a Zika virus?

How can a gun protect against the Zika virus?
You can shoot it.

You can't shoot a virus with a gun.
Really? Check the Constitution.

How should I carry my firearm while I run? Just, like,

in my hand? Or what?
Carrying your gun in your hand at all times is optimal, because what if you need to shoot something immediately? Do you really want to have to reach all the way down to a holster or waistband before you're able to provide yourself and those around you with protection?

On a related note, when holding your gun during a run, be sure not to swing the arm holding the gun. Keep it, and the gun, pointed straight out in front of you. Just in case.

Better still is to continuously and slowly rotate yourself, arm and gun outstretched. This is called "lighthousing" and it gives you a full 360 degrees of protection. Though it can be tough to do while running.

But what if I need both hands while I'm running? To text a friend, for instance?
In cases like those, I guess you *could* keep your gun in a holster for a few minutes.

What are your thoughts on bras with built-in gun holsters?
They're OK, though women can usually carry them off better than men.

If I'm wearing a bra holster, should I ever try to "adjust" it?
No.[1]

While running, what's better—open carry or concealed carry?

---

[1] In 2015, a Michigan woman did so with tragic consequences.

As stated earlier, your best option really is to hand carry. With duct tape. But this is not always feasible.

The open vs. concealed question is a matter of some debate. Open carry advocates say that the very visibility of a firearm will deter crime while also advertising your love of Freedom and disdain for Tyranny, and definitely won't make you a target for Bad Guys who want your gun and, while they're at it, whatever cash you have plus your phone. The concealed carry crowd argue that it's best to hide your gun so as to keep the Bad Guys guessing.

An increasingly popular solution is to open carry a realistic-looking fake gun while concealing your actual gun. This way, if a Bad Guy grabs your gun it will result in confusion and dismay and while he stands there scratching his head and wondering what's going on you can produce your real gun and shoot him in the face.

Score one for justice!

What if I'm running with my gun duct-taped to my hand but I need to stop and pee?

You'll have to manage with one hand while waving the gun around with the other. (You're especially vulnerable while urinating.)

Can't I just carry some scissors with me, and some extra duct tape, so I can remove the tape before I pee and then re-tape it afterward?

Run with scissors? Are you nuts?

What else can I use my gun for while running?

A gun is a surprisingly versatile tool, like one of those Leatherman things that dads get for Father's Day. In addition to keeping Bad Guys in check, runners can use their guns to:

- Shoot down drones
- Crack nuts
- Signal for help if lost in the wilderness
- Start impromptu races
- Open stubborn energy gel packets
- Shoot any other guns they find lying around on the ground, to render them harmless

Do these tips apply to other outdoor fitness enthusiasts as well? Skiers, for instance?
Yes. Yes, they do.[1]

Happy running, runners. And be careful out there.

---

[1] Actual headline from January 2016: "Skier Loses Handgun in Crash at Jackson Hole; Another Skis Over It."

Comedic Genius Runs "Only When Chased"

February 16, 2016

Millions of Americans run. Some do it for fitness and health, others to lose or maintain weight, or to relieve stress, or because they're training for an event such as a marathon. Many regular runners will tell you they run for all of these reasons, and more.

Not so with Colin McDonnell.

McDonnell, 27, a sales rep in Columbus, Ohio, has one motivation for running, and one motivation only.

"I only run when chased," he says.

If you haven't already guessed, McDonnell is also a world-class funnyman.

"Colin never fails to crack me up," says Laura Pettigrew, a runner who works with McDonnell. "I can still remember when I was hired and introduced to the rest of the team. My boss knew I'd recently run a half-marathon, so he mentioned this to a few people, including Colin."

"He didn't miss a beat," recalls Pettigrew. "He shook my hand and said, 'Runner, huh? I only run when chased.' The entire office just collapsed, we were laughing so hard."

"I remember thinking, *Oh, I'll have to watch out for this one—he's trouble!*"

Humor experts say that McDonnell's joke resonates so

strongly because of the mental image it conjures—that of a man who dislikes running so much, he will engage in the activity only if he's faced with an immediate threat to his well-being.

"You can just picture it, can't you?" says Richard Whitcomb, Ph.D., director of the Center for Humor and Comedy Research in Intercourse, Pennsylvania. "A grown man, an avowed non-runner, is going along, minding his own business, when suddenly he realizes someone is pursuing him. And he thinks to himself, *Yikes! Okay, now I'll run!* It's priceless."

The "chase" gag isn't the only arrow in McDonnell's comedic quiver, however.

"Last fall I traveled to New York to run the New York City Marathon," says Pettigrew, the runner and coworker. "When I got back to work the following Tuesday, everyone gathered around to see my medal and congratulate me.

"Not Colin," she says. "Colin strolled up, grinning like the Cheshire Cat, and asked, 'Did you win?'

"Well, let's just say none of us got much work done that morning. We were too busy howling. Eventually the folks in accounting came down the hall and asked us to quiet down.

"I slapped my thigh so much that day, I actually bruised it."

What's next for McDonnell? The wisecracking wunderkind will say only that he's "working on something big."

"All I can tell you," he says, flashing his trademark grin, "is that it involves me and how I feel after just *driving* 26 miles."

The Ugly Side of "Nice Guy" Meb Keflezighi

February 18, 2016

Meb Keflezighi is a living legend, and rightfully so. A three-time Olympian (and winner of a Silver Medal at the 2004 Games in Athens), the 40-year-old Keflezighi counts marathon wins at Boston and New York City among his many accomplishments. Last weekend he finished second at the U.S. Olympic Marathon Trials in Los Angeles, earning a spot on his fourth U.S. Olympic team.

He's famous for other reasons, too. The father of three has a reputation not just as a fierce competitor but as, well, a nice guy. Soft-spoken and quick to smile, Keflezighi is unfailingly polite, gracious, and humble in interviews and public appearances.

What most people don't know is that there's another side to Meb. Through interviews with ordinary people who have crossed his path over the years, Dumb Runner has heard several stories that paint a very different picture. And it's not a pretty one.

Here are just a few of their anecdotes.

Not a Kind Man

"Tom" (names have been changed throughout) was working as a clerk at a Los Angeles Blockbuster video store in 1987 when, as he recalls, a young Meb Keflezighi walked in and returned some videos.

"He seemed nice and normal," Tom says. "But it was all a facade. After he left, I opened the boxes to check the tapes. I couldn't believe my eyes. Despite the prominent 'Be Kind, Rewind' sticker affixed to each of our VHS tapes, he had not rewound one of his videos."

Even today, Tom says, the memory gives him chills.

"He's more monster than man," he says. "I mean, what kind of person doesn't rewind?"

No Respect for the Rule of Law

We are a society of laws. Unless, that is, you're Meb Keflezighi.

"Back in the day, I delivered at least 500 sleep slabs," says Jake, who, as a young man, put himself through college delivering mattresses. "That's what we called 'em in the biz—sleep slabs."

It was good money, Jake says, and pretty uneventful work. Until one day he and his partner rang the doorbell of one Meb Keflezighi.

"Everything was fine at first," recalls Jake. "But once we got his mattress upstairs, things got weird. He noticed the tag on the mattress—you know, the one that says DO NOT REMOVE UNDER PENALTY OF LAW?—and he started touching it, with this diabolical look in his eyes."

What happened next shook Jake to his core.

"He removed that tag."

Jake quit his job that afternoon.

"You see something like that, you just can't unsee it," he says. "I went back to the warehouse, turned in my back brace, and walked away from mattress delivery forever."

Keeps the Change

The idea behind those ubiquitous Take a Penny/Leave a Penny trays is simple—if you could use a penny or two when paying for your lotto ticket and beef jerky, you take them; if you have a penny or two left over, you leave them for the next guy.

Apparently Meb Keflezighi never got that memo.

"I was behind Meb in line at the 7-Eleven," says Gus, a resident of Mammoth Lakes, California, where Keflezighi used to train. "I can't remember what he was buying, but I do remember how he paid for it—with cash, including not one, not two, but three pennies from the Take a Penny/Leave a Penny tray. One, two, three. Boom, boom, boom."

The entire store fell silent, Gus says.

"I was stunned. Later, I asked my Facebook friends if anyone had ever seen Meb leave a penny, much less three. The silence was deafening.

"I never pegged Meb as a selfish, entitled dude. You never can tell, I guess."

Too 'Busy' for a Photo

"I'd always been a big fan of Meb's," says Judy, a recreational runner and mother of two. "So I was beyond excited when I spotted him in Boston, the weekend of the 2014 Boston Marathon. It was right around mile 25."

"I held up my phone and leaned over the barrier to ask if I could get a selfie with him," she says. "It was like he didn't even hear me. He just kept right on running. Not so much as a glance in my direction.

"It was unbelievable," she continues. "I mean, he had at least 10 seconds on the guy behind him. At least. More than enough time for a quick photo with a fan. What do you tell your kids after something like that?

"I thought Meb was different from all these other snooty pro athletes. Guess not.

"I just don't know what to believe anymore."

Kitten Runs Marathon to Raise Awareness of Own Cuteness

February 23, 2016

Road races these days are full of people running for a cause, typically to raise money for charity. Last weekend's Trumbull County (Ohio) Marathon was no exception. Runners with the Leukemia & Lymphoma Society's Team in Training were out in force, wearing their trademark purple shirts, as were groups and individuals running for any number of good causes.

Among that event's 4,500 or so entrants, however, was a runner with a very atypical goal—to raise awareness of his own cuteness.

That entrant was Mr. Wuffles, an orange tabby kitten. And by any measure, he met his goal in a big way.

"Oh, my God," said Rebecca Raymond, 43, who spotted the 8-week-old feline in the race's starting corral. "He's wearing a tiny headband. That is *adorable*." (Mr. Wuffles would later lose his headband, which in fact was a human terrycloth wristband, somewhere in the race's first few miles.)

"So cute," agreed her friend and training partner, also named Rebecca Raymond. "Oh, my God. Look."

Spectators along the course said they, too, noticed Mr. Wuffles, despite the fact that his tiny, soft body is small enough to curl up into a soup bowl.

"Oh, my God," said Timothy Hempstead, 30, who was waiting at mile 12 for his wife to run by. "Is that a kitten? With a little bib number? That is *so cute*."

Even local law enforcement stationed along the course couldn't resist Mr. Wuffles' brisk little stride and big, innocent-looking eyes.

"Oh, my God," said Officer Chris Torres, 52, as Mr. Wuffles shuffled past. "That is the cutest ****ing thing I have ever seen."

Mr. Wuffles seems to have run the entire way, except for one bathroom break at the halfway point, which witnesses described as "so cute," and around 30 occasions where he was sidetracked by small birds, bouncing shoelaces, and, at one point, a rubber band lying on the road.

Reports that Mr. Wuffles trained for the race in part on a cute, tiny treadmill could not be confirmed.

Race volunteers reportedly fought one another to scoop Mr. Wuffles up at aid stations to give him a little drink of water and a scritch under the chin before seeing him off to continue his race.

"Oh, my God," said Chrissy Valentine, 19, a volunteer at the mile 22 aid station. "Like, oh, my God."

"So cute," she added.

The praise wasn't entirely universal.

"The whole thing looks to me like a cheap stunt," said Becca Raymond. (No relation to the previous two Raymonds.) "I don't know who's behind it, but using cute animals to attract attention is totally lame."

"It's like tossing a cat video or kitten photos into an otherwise stupid blog post or something, just to get people to click and share it," she continued. "Laziest ploy in the world."

Asked what was next on his race calendar, Mr. Wuffles rolled onto his back and batted at some fluffy, white dandelion florets floating by on the breeze.

"Oh, my God," said a passerby who paused to watch. "That is so cute."

Studies Show Music Can Boost Your Running, Right Up to the Moment You're Struck by a Car That You Couldn't Hear

March 18, 2016

You already know that running is just more enjoyable with music. But did you know it can actually improve your performance?

From PsychologyToday.com:

An expert in the psychology of exercise, Costas Karageorghis, Ph.D., refers to music as a "type of legal performance-enhancing drug" for its potent abilities to increase productivity as well as power and strength.

Dr. Karageorghis and other researchers have long studied the effects of music on exercise, and the verdict is in: In addition to motivating you, music can make you a faster and stronger runner until a sudden, catastrophic injury leaves you injured or dead.

"This is really exciting news," says Gregory Newsome, vice president of sports marketing for Apple, maker of music players popular among runners. "And it confirms what we've believed all along—that music is indeed a powerful tool in the runner's toolbox. A tool that can be used to great effect, until you're hit by a car or truck that you couldn't hear coming."

What music is best for runners? Dr. Karageorghis recommends tunes with a tempo between 120 and 140 beats per minute, such as "Push It" by Salt-N-Pepa or "Drop It Like It's Hot" by Snoop Dogg. These will "pump you up" and keep your pace high until the hand of fate reaches out and strikes you hard when you least expect it.

Listening to up-tempo music, Dr. Karageorghis says, will "enhance affect, reduce ratings of perceived exertion, improve energy efficiency, and lead to increased work output," until everything goes black and your music player goes flying and skitters across the macadam as a result of a motor vehicle collision that might easily have been avoided if you hadn't chosen to dull your sense of hearing while running on public streets and roads.

Anecdotal evidence appears to back this up.

"Before I got my MP3 player, runs were just drudgery," says Rhonda Chang, 22, a student in Austin, Texas. "When I began listening to music, though, *wow*. The difference was amazing. My pace picked up, and the miles just rolled by. It was great, right up to the moment I got hit by a bus that I never heard.

"Guess I was really in the zone!"

Chang expects to be walking normally again as early as this fall.

She isn't alone.

"John loved his running playlist," says Becky Evanston, 28, whose husband was an avid runner until an accident last summer left him in a medically induced coma. "He wouldn't go for a run without his music. Said it really motivated him.

"I like to think he was running along, rocking out to Daft Punk or U2, when he ran through that intersection and got hit. He loved Daft Punk and U2. Sometimes I sit and hold his hand and play it for him."

When her husband emerges from his coma, which she is sure he will any day now, Becky predicts the first thing he'll do is ask about the latest music so he can update his running playlist.

"He can't run without his tunes," she says.

How to Choose a Porta Potty That *Doesn't* Have a Penis-Biting Spider

April 27, 2016

As we have said many times before, readers, this world is full of threats. This is why we recommend you always carry a loaded gun with you everywhere you go—especially when you're out for a run.[1] All it takes is one moment of letting down your guard for disaster to strike.

An Australian man learned this lesson the hard way Tuesday when he ducked into a portable toilet to relieve himself (presumably without a weapon—thanks, strict gun laws!) and was bitten on the penis by a venomous redback spider.

We could go on in more detail about this incident, but really, what more is there to say? A spider bit a guy. On the penis. In a porta potty.

We will offer this bit of trivia, though, from a report on AdelaideNow.com.au:

... Associate Professor Julian White from Adelaide's Women's and Children's Hospital ... said minor bites were common in Australia.

"Going back 80 years or so when people were still using outhouse

---

[1] See "Running With Your Gun: FAQ," page 16.

toilets it was extremely common, something like up to 80 percent of cases of spider bites were bites on the male genitalia," he said.

Which is good to know.

As a runner who has used probably hundreds of porta potties in my day, I'd say that being bitten on the penis by a venomous spider was my worst nightmare, except that it's so insane it never occurred to me to have nightmares about it. Until now.

It's too late for the poor bastard in Australia. (He is reportedly in "stable condition" and expected to go home soon.) But not for you. The next time you're at an event and need to use a portable toilet, keep these tips in mind:

Introduce several spider wasps into the potty before you use it. Preferably the species *Agenioideus nigricornis*. According to Wikipedia, here's what will happen to any redback spiders unlucky enough to be in there:

A female wasp will search ... for a spider, and upon finding one, will sting it, paralyzing the spider. Once the spider is paralyzed, the female wasp makes a burrow or takes the spider to a previously made burrow. She lays a single egg on the abdomen of the spider using her ovipositor, and then encloses the spider in the burrow. The egg will hatch and the larva will feed on the spider, breaking through the integument with its mandibles.

Once you can verify that any spiders in there are indeed paralyzed and being consumed by your wasps' larva, you'll know it's safe to use the porta potty.

Send someone in to do some recon. You've trained hard for this event. Why should you risk it all just to take a leak? Find someone nearby to scout ahead and check the porta potty for venomous spiders before you go in. In fact, try to use an actual Scout. Boy or Girl, doesn't matter. Tell them it counts toward their Insect Study Merit Badge.

Put yourself in the spider's shoes. To defeat the redback spider, one must become the redback spider. Look at the row of porta potties before you and ask yourself, *If I were a redback spider, in which one would I choose to spin my web?* Then don't go into that one.

Choose one porta potty and watch the guys emerging from it. If they appear normal and healthy, it's probably clear. If they shriek as they come crashing through the door, clutching their red, inflamed genitalia and screaming, "That spider just bit my penis!" you'll want to opt for another one.

Just pee in your pants. This may be your best, safest option. Honestly.

Study: "1-Minute Workouts" Useless When It Comes to Shit You Can't Quantify

May 3, 2016

High-intensity training is once again in the news, thanks to a recent study suggesting that a 60-second burst of intense exercise can, as *The New York Times* puts it, be "as successful at improving health and fitness as three-quarters of an hour of moderate exercise."

The study, titled "Twelve Weeks of Sprint Interval Training Improves Indices of Cardiometabolic Health Similar to Traditional Endurance Training despite a Five-Fold Lower Exercise Volume and Time Commitment,"[1] is just the latest in a string of studies touting the benefits of interval training—good news, the *Times* says, for those of us wondering, *How little [exercise] can I get away with?*

A different team of researchers, however, has just released its own findings on the subject. That team's conclusion: Such "1-minute workouts" are, in their words, "utterly worthless when it comes to the shit that can't be measured, which in this life is some of the most important shit of all.

"For real," they add.

---

[1] Study authors: I am available for editing assignments. Call me.

These researchers, led by Dr. Cleavon Little of the Global Happiness Institute in Stockholm, followed a group of 96 healthy adults. Most of those adults soon got creeped out and asked the team to stop following them, so Dr. Little and his researchers recruited a fresh batch of subjects.

These were split into two groups. Half engaged three times weekly in the sort of 60-second interval workouts used in the previously cited study; the other half instead did trail runs on those days, each 40 to 60 minutes in duration and done at a fairly easy pace.

After 12 weeks, both groups were tested.

The interval-training group, as expected, showed significant gains in peak oxygen uptake, insulin resistance, and various things that can be measured in units like "milliliters of oxygen per minute per kilogram of body weight." They also, on average, had a little more time each week to tweet and browse Amazon.com and stuff.

The trail-running group exhibited the same or nearly the same physiological gains as the first group. But, the researchers discovered, their activity yielded some remarkable additional benefits.

"Specifically," said Dr. Little, "their souls were healthier. They were happier and more at peace and much more likely to report having noticed something really cool, like a hawk. In essence, they felt better about themselves, life, and the universe."

Why?

"This is just a wild hunch," Dr. Little said, "but we think it's because they were outside running and breathing and living instead of, you know, engaging in some grim, frantic attempt to 'improve indices of cardiometabolic health' in the shortest amount of time possible because they've bought into this notion that health and fitness can be reduced to tables of data, that exercise—otherwise known as 'moving'—is awful and something to be avoided or minimized, and that 'no one has time' to exercise even though the average American watches nearly three hours of TV a day.

"Again," Dr. Little added, "just a hunch."

In conclusion, Dr. Little's study determined, "Take half an hour and go for a run. For f***'s sake."

Mythical "5K Marathon" May Be Real, Researchers Say

May 9, 2016

In a stunning discovery, scientists at the Massachusetts Institute of Research have announced that the 5K marathon, long thought to be a legend, may in fact be an actual race distance.

"We're very excited," said Daniel Partridge, Ph.D., who led the effort. "Until now we'd assumed the 5K marathon was a mythical construct, a fable. Something that people liked to talk about but that, of course, didn't exist—sort of the Loch Ness Monster of the road racing universe."

Like everyone else, they also assumed logically that a 5K marathon was a mathematical impossibility. After all, a 5K by definition is 3.1 miles; a marathon, 26.2. The very term *5K marathon*, then, would seem paradoxical.

But through sophisticated computer modeling and quantum mechanics, and with "an awful lot of trial and error," Dr. Partridge and his assistants made their breakthrough last week.

"We were surprised, to say the least," Dr. Partridge said. "We checked our work two, three, four times. But there it was—the very real possibility that 5K marathons do indeed exist.

"And not just on Earth, either," he added.

Partridge said his colleagues congratulated him on his

discovery by spraying him with bottles of Lemon-Lime Gatorade.

Other groups, too, were celebrating.

"Finally, vindication," said Ann B. Davis, a spokesperson for the National Association of Newspaper Reporters, a trade group. "We've been mentioning 5K marathons in our articles for years, and it's earned us nothing but ridicule. It is gratifying to learn that maybe we knew what we were talking about all along."

Dr. Partridge, known as a tireless worker with a restless intellect, already has his sights on the horizon.

"The next logical step," he said, "is to prove the existence of the 10K marathon."

But first, perhaps, will he celebrate? By running a 5K marathon, maybe?

Dr. Partridge laughed.

"No, no, no," he said. "I don't run. Bad for the knees."

Dumb Runner Travel Alert: Australia

May 18, 2016

Readers, I am sorry to barge into your normal, quiet day with alarming news. But I feel duty-bound to tell you, in all caps, that UNDER NO CIRCUMSTANCES SHOULD YOU TRAVEL TO AUSTRALIA.

UNLESS YOU ENJOY BEING HIT BY AIRBORNE KANGAROOS WHILE OUT FOR A RUN.

I.E., WHEN YOU ARE OUT FOR A RUN. NOT WHEN THE KANGAROOS ARE OUT FOR A RUN.

YOU KNOW WHAT WE MEAN.

This advisory comes as Dumb Runner is learning of a recent so-called "accident" in—we are not making this up—Kangaroo Flat, a small town about 90 miles northwest of Melbourne.

According to a report on TheAge.com.au:

A jogger out for a predawn run has been injured after a car slammed into a kangaroo, flipping the animal into him.

Sam Walter, 28, said the bizarre collision might have been karma for his choice of dinner on Tuesday night—kangaroo steak.

He sustained leg injuries when the kangaroo was propelled toward him "like a football" by the impact.

We will pause once more to reiterate that this is an actual news story.

We are still struggling to get our heads around this story. Here is what we've been able to determine so far:

- Apparently some people eat kangaroo steak.
- According to Wikipedia, "Kangaroo Flat is home to the Kangaroos Football and Netball team." It is unclear whether this is just a name, or the team is composed of actual kangaroos. We desperately hope it's the latter, because could you imagine a bunch of kangaroos in uniforms?
- In the state of Victoria (which includes Kangaroo Flat), kangaroos topped the list of animals cited in car insurance claims last year. They were involved in eight of 10 such accidents.
- Wombats came in at number two. (Seriously.)
- Thirty years after *Crocodile Dundee*, we still cannot hear or read a story about Australia without thinking automatically of Paul Hogan. "G'day!" Does this happen to anyone else?
- Paul Hogan, it turns out, married *Dundee* costar Linda Kozlowski in 1990. They are now divorced and, it was reported just this month, he is "ridding his L.A. home of all traces of his ex-wife—including the iconic red dress she wore in *Crocodile Dundee*." Well, that's sad.

There is still much we don't know. We therefore think you should stay put for the time being and not travel to Australia. Between this and the penis-biting spiders they have down there,[1] the risk is just not worth it.

If you're reading this in an airplane en route to Australia, you may deplane when you land—but *do not leave*

---

[1] See "How to Choose a Porta Potty That *Doesn't* Have a Penis-Biting Spider," page 33.

the airport. Await the next flight home and get yourself on it. Even if that means stowing away in a wheel well. Because flying a few thousand miles in an unpressurized jumbo jet wheel well is a picnic compared with being hit by a flying kangaroo, believe us.

In fact, we will go a step further. Dumb Runner is calling for a total and complete shutdown of kangaroos entering the United States until our country's representatives can figure out what the hell is going on.

Stay safe, folks.

Awful Things That Could Bite Your Genitals in the Toilet, Ranked

May 27, 2016

Readers, we never thought it would come to this. But it appears that "Things That Could Bite Your Genitals in the Toilet" has gone from wacky, one-off story to full-blown actual trend.

The wacky, one-off story, as regular Dumb Runner readers will know, concerned a man in Australia who walked into a porta potty to relieve himself only to achieve the opposite of relief, in the form of a bite from a venomous redback spider.

On his penis.[1]

Well, we all had a good laugh about that. All of us except the victim, we guess. And the spider, who is incapable of laughter, which is really very sad if you think about it.

No one is laughing now. Because now we have a second confirmed case of a man being bitten on his penis while sitting on a toilet.

This time, though, the biter wasn't a spider. It was a

---

[1] See—again!—"How to Choose a Porta Potty That *Doesn't* Have a Penis-Biting Spider," page 33.

python.

Now, you might have seen this story yourself and misinterpreted it if you only read the headline. The headline used by the *Daily Mail*, for instance, reads:

Python Sinks Its Fangs Into Man's Penis
as He Sits on the Toilet

Which creates confusion right off the bat. Who is sitting on the toilet? The python? The man? You just don't know.

When you click to read the article, of course, you learn that it's the man who was sitting when the python bite occurred. We'll spare you the details, except to say that the victim was a 38-year-old Thai man, that the incident happened in his home, and that "after feeling a sharp bite," he reached down "to discover the serpent's jaws clamped around the tip of his penis." Also, the python was 11 feet long.

Actually, that was quite a lot of details. Oh well. At least we didn't show you the photos.[1]

The point, readers, is that this is now officially a huge threat. Not just because a second man has had his junk bitten while using the toilet in recent weeks, but because apparently we aren't safe even in our own homes.

We mean, you walk into a porta potty, you almost expect something in there to bite you in your bikini area. But in your own house?

Also, things appear to be trending in a very bad direction. First there was a spider bite. Next, a python. What's next? Could things possibly get worse?

We don't know, but we've been giving this a lot of

---

[1] My God, the photos.

thought and we have developed what we think is a pretty solid list of the Worst Things That Might Bite Your Genitals in the Toilet.

1. Puppy
Sure, he looks cute. But his jaws are surprisingly strong and those teeth are like tiny X-acto knives.

2. Candiru Fish
This small, parasitic fish has a "supposed habit of entering the human penis, lodging itself in place with sharp barbs, and feasting on it from the inside."[1] Reportedly by swimming "upstream" as its victim urinates. Many question whether such an attack has ever actually happened, but, man... You can imagine, right?

3. Young Bornean Orangutan in Glasses and Bow Tie

---

[1] So says Wikipedia.

Being bitten on the penis by a young Bornean orangutan wearing glasses and a bow tie would be painful not just physically but emotionally. He's wearing glasses and a bow tie. You thought you could trust him.

4. Llama

First of all, have you ever seen a llama's teeth? Second, llamas always look filthy. And finally, llamas spit. Imagine a llama biting your penis when you're at your most vulnerable—and then spitting at you. Way to add insult to injury, dirty llama.

5. Mrs. Benson, Your Old Kindergarten Teacher

Eww! What's she even doing in there, anyway? And what's with that camera?

6. Hurst S 700 CutterHSS "Jaws of Life" 10,000 PSI Cutter

According to the manufacturer, "The S 700's extrication

capabilities ... include shipboard damage control, structural collapse, aircraft egress, and plenty of other tough situations." Just imagine what it could do to your genitals. Oh, you'd rather not? Yeah. That's what we thought.

7. Mosquito
OK, the bite itself might not hurt. But the itching!

Copernicus Is First Renaissance Mathematician and Astronomer to Grace Cover of *Women's Running* Magazine

June 20, 2016

Women's Running magazine will feature a groundbreaking circa-16th-century scientist on its cover this September—a move that is being hailed as "overdue" and "a game changer in the world of publishing."

The magazine today released an image of the cover to media outlets.

Nicolaus Copernicus, an astronomer and mathematician best remembered for introducing the concept of a heliocentric solar system—i.e., one in which the planets revolve around the sun, not around the earth, as most believed in his time—was a logical choice, said Joan Marie Larkin, a spokesperson for the magazine.

"He literally changed the way we look at our place in the universe," said Larkin. "And he did it at a time when doing so could get you in big trouble.

"Copernicus's strength, courage, and can-do attitude make him a perfect cover subject for us and for women runners everywhere," she added.

The famed polymath and polyglot, who lived from 1473 to 1543, possessed a restless and tireless intellect, studying law, medicine, and economics in addition to math and astronomy. His model of a heliocentric solar system, while brilliant, earned him condemnation from many, including the Roman Catholic Church, which called it heretical.

It is unknown whether he was a runner.

Reaction among the magazine's audience was mostly positive.

"OMG yasss I love me some Copernicus," wrote one woman on *Women's Running*'s Facebook page.

"Who?" wrote another.

The September issue hits newsstands on August 8.

7 Ways Runners Can Celebrate Canada Day

July 1, 2016

"It's Canada Day! It's Canada Day!"

That is what runners all over the world shouted when they awoke this morning, waking their neighbors and causing their sleeping spouses and partners to bolt upright in a panic.

And then they paused.

"But what, as a runner, can I do to honor this special day?" they said, also in a shout for some reason. We respect your desire to mark this "federal statutory holiday celebrating the anniversary of the July 1, 1867, enactment of the Constitution Act, 1867 (then called the British North America Act, 1867), which united three colonies into a single country called Canada within the British Empire."[1] And we want to help.

Here are seven ways that runners can celebrate *Fête du Canada*.[2]

1. Cover Your Genitals With Canada's Flag
Go to your local running store and ask to purchase a pair

---

[1] Thanks again, Wikipedia!

[2] French: Literally, "Fête of Canada."

of Canadian flag running shorts. If the staff isn't sure what you're talking about, explain that the shorts in question will look like the Canadian flag—i.e., a plain white field with a pair of Canadian flag running shorts on it.

Then wear the shorts.

2. Measure Today's Run in Kilometers
It'll sound more impressive, anyway. And remember: Every mile you run brings you 1.6 kilometers closer to your goal.[1]

3. Enjoy a Big Slice of Canada Pie
Canada's "national dessert," Canada Pie is basically just regular pie but with a little Canadian flag toothpick stuck in the middle. Canada Pie is traditionally eaten without hands or utensils, like in a pie-eating contest.

4. Wear a Canadian Flag Temporary Tattoo
You know, like the kind you see Canadian runners wearing in American marathons and stuff.

5. Get a Permanent Canadian Flag Tattoo
If you're feeling really committed, why not show it? You could also get a tattoo like the one Prime Minister Justin Trudeau has on his shoulder. Or a tattoo of Prime Minister Justin Trudeau.

---

[1] As seen on Dumb Runner Motivational Poster #8.

6. Acquire This Sweatshirt

Because nothing says "Canadian pride" like wearing a sweatshirt[1] showing Justin Trudeau looking dreamy and riding a horse.

7. Contact Your Representatives in Congress and Demand a National Single-Payer Health Care System

Bonus points if you do so while wearing your Justin Trudeau sweatshirt.

Happy birthday, Canada!

---

[1] Available at Shelfies.com: http://bit.ly/2B7Nr0G

Olympic Runner Admits Doping With Jesus

August 22, 2016

In what's believed to be a first in the world of doping, an Olympic athlete has openly admitted to using Jesus Christ as a performance enhancer.

"My doping is Jesus," Ethiopian runner Almaz Ayana said in an article on ChristianTimes.com:

Ayana had been dogged by rumors of doping ever since she won the 10,000 meters on Friday, August 12—only her second 10,000m race ever—in 29:17.45, smashing a 23-year-old world record in the process. And she had been just as adamant in denying them—until recently.

According to the ChristianTimes.com article, Ayana "named three factors behind her success and even admitted to the allegations of doping—but of a rather unusual kind."

"Three things," she said through a translator. "Number

one, I did my training, Number two, I praise the Lord; He is giving me everything, everything, everything."

Critics immediately pointed out that that is just two things, not three, and speculated that such innumeracy may be a side effect of long-term Jesus use.

Even in an era of rampant doping among elite athletes—including other cases at the Rio Games—Ayana's confession still managed to shock.

"It just goes to show that the fight against doping in athletics is a game of cat and mouse," said Tony Montana, head of the Global Anti-Doping Initiative. "EPO, CERA, human growth hormone, and now, Jesus of Nazareth."

"You develop better screening tests and they just move on to something else," he said. "It's frustrating."

Ayana's competitors were more blunt.

"It's incredible," said one track and field athlete, who requested anonymity. "Using EPO or steroids is one thing. But employing the grace and strength of Our Savior, the Lord Jesus Christ, in order to gain an edge? That's a new low."

"Son of David, Son of Man, Son of God," she continued. "Whatever you call Him, He belongs in church, not on the track, giving certain athletes an unfair advantage."

Ayana's confession also put renewed focus on an earlier incident in Rio, regarding a curious delivery to the Athletes Village. A large, heavy box had arrived for Ayana; concerned by its heft and lack of a return address, security screeners opened it.

The box was full of Bibles.

"It seemed strange, but we sent it along to her room," said Manny Ribera, one of the staff who examined the box. "When Ayana's coach saw it had been opened, he freaked. 'Those aren't our Bibles,' he told us. 'I have no idea who those belong to.'

"He was sweating, very nervous. It seemed weird at the time."

The International Olympic Committee says it is studying the case and will not rule out stripping Ayana of her Gold Medal. In the meantime, anti-doping officials say they will work to develop a test to detect the presence of the Holy Spirit in an athlete's system.

Elevated levels of salvation aren't proof of cheating, said Montana, of the Global Anti-Doping Initiative.

"But it certainly raises red flags."

Local Runner Worried She'll Never Crush a Race

August 31, 2016

By most any measure, Jan Brady seems to have it all.

The local 36-year-old, a physician, has a thriving practice and two young children. She's active in the community, volunteering at food pantries and coaching a local school's cross-country team. Brady herself is an avid runner, having completed four marathons and countless shorter races, from 5Ks to half-marathons.

Still, she says, there's one thing missing—and it haunts her, day and night.

"I've been a runner for seven years," she says, "and I have never crushed a race. Not once."

Brady is quick to acknowledge her running

accomplishments—her personal record for the marathon is a very respectable 3 hours and 17 minutes—and to express gratitude for a long, healthy career as a runner. She's equally open in pointing to races that she has "nailed" and PRs that she has "smashed" or "shattered."

But after seven years, she has yet to "crush" a race. Of any distance.

"At this point," she says, laughing, "I'd be happy just to crush a 5K. I don't care what race I crush, as long as I crush it."

Experts say Brady's experience is not uncommon. As many as 15% of runners will never crush a race. Often a genetic defect may be to blame—in simple terms, some of us are just incapable of crushing a race. Other times, it comes down to bad luck.

"There are so many variables that factor into crushing a race," explains Sam Franklin, Ph.D., a professor of exercise science at the University of Minnesota. "Most of us, if we keep at it long enough, will hit that combination at least once. A few of us simply won't."

Whatever the reason, Brady says, she finds it hard to cope. She stopped using Facebook about a year ago, finding her news feed too much to bear.

"It was full of friends' race reports and finishing times," she says. "They were all crushing it. I was happy for them, but every single post hit me like a dagger."

Still, Brady says she's hanging in there and trying to stay positive.

"I'm hopeful," she says. "Every time I toe the line, I think, *This could be the race I crush*. I just keep telling myself that running isn't about self-pity. It's about perseverance.

"I got this."

70% of Americans Unable to Locate "Core" on Map of Body

October 3, 2016

Seven in 10 Americans can't locate the "core" on a human body, a new survey says.

The news is surprising, experts say, considering how often we're urged to strengthen, tighten, tone, target, challenge, sculpt, activate, rock, or blast our cores.

The survey, conducted in shopping malls across the country, included 2,800 subjects divided roughly equally between men and women. While three in 10, asked to locate the "core" on a diagram of the human body, correctly pointed to the lumbo-pelvic-hip complex, which involves deeper muscles, such as the internal oblique, transversus abdominis, transversospinalis (multifidus, rotatores, semispinalis), quadratus lumborum, and psoas major and minor, and superficial muscles, such as the rectus abdominis, external oblique, erector spinae (iliocostalis, spinalis, longissimus), latissimus dorsi, gluteus maximus and medius, hamstrings, and rectus femoris, the remainder of subjects either guessed incorrectly or just stood and stared at the interviewer, chewing slowly on a Cinnabon.

The research was undertaken by the National Council on Core Strength, an association of personal trainers, kettlebell manufacturers, and magazine headline writers.

The next step, they say, is a public education campaign.

"The core is crucial, bro," said Zach Bradford, 24, chief researcher, from the floor, where he was doing bird-dog crunches. "You gotta have a strong core."

"And you can't blast your core if you don't know where to blast," added Cassie Sprinkles, 27, a personal trainer who was performing Swiss ball jackknifes nearby.

"You use your core every time you bend, turn, or lift!" they then shouted in unison.

Some other key findings from the research:

- 11% of respondents think the core is a part of the brain.
- 24%, when asked to find the core, pointed to the genital region.
- 30% asked the interviewer whether they were giving out free samples.
- 6% volunteered that they had recently had a "core smoothie."

The researchers say the results are discouraging, but they're committed to spreading the message of core strength.

"6 Easy Exercises to Strengthen Your Core," said Jeff Hurkins, a magazine writer. "13 Essential Core Exercises for Runners."

27 Anagrams of *Chicago Marathon*

October 5, 2016

This Sunday, about 40,000 runners will "lace up their sneakers," "toe the line," and "hit the streets" for the 2016 Bank of America® "Thank God We Turned Down That Wells Fargo® Sponsorship Offer" Chicago Marathon®.

If you'll be running the race—or maybe even if you won't be—you probably have lots of questions. Questions like, "Who's in the elite field this year?" and "Will I be able to watch Sunday's race online?" and "Where can I find advice on running the Chicago Marathon that includes the phrase *coked-up rhino*?"[1]

Most crucially, you are probably asking, "Can you make any good anagrams out of the letters in *Chicago Marathon*?"

Readers, Dumb Runner is here to help.

The answers to those first three questions are, well… right up there. That's what the hyperlinks are for. It's 2016, guys. Do we really need to explain how hyperlinks work?[2]

For the answer to that final question we turned to the Internet Anagram Server. The answer is: Yes. Yes, you can make many good anagrams out of the letters in *Chicago*

---

[1] In the *Chicago Tribune*, as it turned out.

[2] They do not work in books. ☹

Marathon.

Here are 27 of them.

1. Harmonica Cat Hog
2. Marching Cahoot
3. Maraca Chino Goth
4. Anarchic Moot Hag
5. Archaic Math Goon
6. Hot Carcinoma Hag
7. Got Carcinoma? Hah!
8. Chairman Taco Hog
9. Maniac Roach Goth
10. Macaroni Chat Hog
11. Macaroon Hag Itch
12. Tarmac Aching Ooh
13. A Garmin Hooch Cart
14. Hootch Cram? Again?
15. Aroma Gotcha Chin
16. Thoracic Hag Moan
17. Chaotic Groan Ham
18. Caroming Taco! Hah
19. Racing Ham Cahoot
20. Organic Macho Hat
21. Harmonic Taco Hag
22. Ooh, A Marching Act
23. A Charming Taco? Oh
24. Hoo! A Racing Match
25. Macho Orca Hating
26. A Moth Hair Cognac
27. Gotcha Mocha Rain

Good luck to everyone running Chicago this weekend!

Cute Running Couple Are Just So Perfect in Their Little Running Outfits

October 16, 2016

Numerous sources are reporting that a local running couple are just so cute and perfect, running around in their little stylish running clothes.

The man and woman, as yet unidentified, have been spotted jogging together on the multi-use path, running along the riverfront, on adjoining treadmills at the gym, and at the Starbucks across from the Pottery Barn, playfully dabbing whipped cream on each other's noses.

"They're always together, always happy," said Peter

Gabriel, a local runner who recently saw the couple laughing and stretching together on a downtown street corner. "And they always just look so... perfect. In their cute little running outfits."

They also reportedly often interrupt their workouts to glance at each other and exchange coy grins.

While some details vary from sighting to sighting—her hairstyle, for example, or the heaviness of his stubble—sources say the couple's appearance is remarkably predictable.

"I've never seen them *not* look put together," said Jane Smith, another local runner. "They're always wearing these perfect little outfits—usually Lululemon or Nike stuff, though sometimes she'll be in Oiselle. It all looks brand-new. I can only imagine what their closets look like.

"Also, I swear, they don't sweat. Ever."

Beyond that, little is known about the couple.

"I'd guess they're in their mid-20s," said Philip Collins, a barista at the Starbucks the couple often visits post-run. "Or well-preserved 30-somethings.

"Actually," he continued, "that wouldn't surprise me at all. You can just tell these guys take care of themselves and probably get a solid eight hours of sleep a night, probably on freshly laundered, lavender-scented sheets, and use expensive soaps, with charcoal or tea tree oil or something, and skin-care products from Kiehl's."

"I bet they have amazing sex, too. In their cute little apartment, with a bright kitchen and hardwood floors and a clawfoot tub and working fireplace. Probably also with a terrace and a little bistro table and chairs where they sit and have their morning espresso. I hate them."

The couple could not be reached for comment.

Woman Runs Entire Marathon While Juggling Career, Family

October 19, 2016

For most people, running a marathon is hard enough—but Samantha Stephens is not most people. The 36-year-old attorney from Akron, Ohio, recently ran a full marathon while juggling her work and home life for the entire race.

Stephens accomplished her feat at last Sunday's Waynesburg (Pennsylvania) Marathon, cheered on by her husband and two children, ages 2 and 5. She finished in a chip time of 3:38:40, maintaining her work-home balance perfectly every step of the way.

"Not once did she fail to pay adequate attention to her family and personal life at the expense of her professional self," said race director Larry Tate. "And vice versa.

"It was amazing, frankly. I don't know how she did it."

Pending verification, Tate said, that will be a new Guinness World Record.

The current record for juggling career and family during a marathon is 3:51:03, held by Agnes Moorehead, a civil engineer and mother of four from Bristol, England—though some questioned that performance, claiming to have spotted Moorehead's nanny assisting her during the race.

Record or not, Stephens said she's happy with her performance. She credits years of training for her success.

"I've been juggling career and family ever since law school," she told reporters shortly after finishing the race. "At this point, it's just second nature."

She then excused herself to give her children a snack.

Runners Pledge to Never Dope, Except for Really Big Races

November 7, 2016

When Gloria Estefan, a 2:43 marathoner for Ecuador, turned pro four years ago, she was aghast at what she calls "the culture of doping."

"So many runners were cheating, so often, it was astounding," she said. "It was almost like, *If you want to compete at the highest levels, you need to do this.*"

She is ashamed to admit, she says today, that she made some poor choices back then.

"I was using EPO, Clenbuterol, ephedrine, blood

transfusions, superfoods[1], you name it," she said. "I am not proud of what I did. But hopefully this makes up for it, a little bit."

The "this" she's talking about is taking the "Run Cleanish" pledge.

Run Cleanish began as a hashtag on Twitter, used by a handful of track and field athletes who are vowing, in the words of an official statement, to "compete pure, using only my own natural ability, without the aid of performance enhancers, unless it's a really big race where there's a lot riding on the outcome."

Since it began about a month ago, the #runcleanish campaign has exploded, attracting hundreds of runners promising in a highly visible and shareable way never to dope except when they really and truly need that little extra something.

Anti-doping officials are applauding the initiative.

"It's very encouraging to see athletes finally taking a proactive step like this," said Frank Drebin, president of the Global Anti-Doping Network.

"For too long, even mediocre competitors felt pressured to use drugs, blood doping, or other banned performance-enhancing techniques," he continued. "Now, finally, they're realizing that they really don't need to, except on a few rare occasions where the results are simply too important to leave to chance."

Others are taking notice, too.

"I think it's a good thing, because drugs are bad," said Andrew Jackson, 8, as he watched yesterday's New York City Marathon on Manhattan's First Avenue. "You should

---

[1] Superfoods!

never, ever take drugs. Unless you really need them to level the playing field."

He paused.

"Mom says I can use Twitter when I'm a little older."

Here's How Runners Can Dodge Trump Talk This Thanksgiving

November 23, 2016

Readers, this year's Thanksgiving comes just two weeks after what was easily the most wrenching, contentious, divisive, polarizing, hysterical, infuriating, nauseating emotional roller coaster of an election in modern American history.

The good news is, that's all behind us.

HAHAHAHAHA! Sorry. Excuse us while we laugh so hard we pee a little bit of blood. Of course that's not behind us.

If anything, the wrenching, contention, division, polarization, hysteria, infuriation, and nausea have all gotten worse, and there's no end in sight. It's like the emotional roller coaster has gone haywire and cannot stop whipping us around and around and around, possibly because it was hacked. (By Russia? Maybe!)

This means that the usual political talk at Thanksgiving will be a lot more unpleasant this year.

Or will it?

As a runner, you probably have a talent for turning just about any conversation into a conversation about running in general, and your running in particular. With a little preparation, you can use this talent to great effect at the

Thanksgiving table.

The trick is to interject immediately upon hearing a potentially explosive remark, redirecting before things have a chance to escalate. Think of it as verbal judo. In between bites of green bean casserole.

To pull this off, you'll need to be prepared. Here are a few lines that might come in handy.

Potentially Explosive Remark: "So. Trump is already backing off his promise to build a wall."
Your Response: "Oh, man! You wanna talk about walls, let me tell you about my last marathon. Everything was fine until around mile 18..."

Potentially Explosive Remark: "Trump is going to make America great again."
Your Response: "Hey! You know what's going great for me? My training. Last week I did these Yasso 800s, and they were just, like, bang! Bang! Bang! Spot-on. Anyway, who wants more sweet potatoes?"

Potentially Explosive Remark: "I can't wait to see how Trump deals with ISIS."
Your Response: "My running buddy ices. Her Achilles, after every run. Like, as a preventative thing. Isn't that crazy? Ha ha! But, I guess if it works for her..."

Potentially Explosive Remark: "Why does everything have to be about race?"
Your Response: "Speaking of races, my turkey trot this morning was pretty great. You guys should really try to make it next year. There's one guy who always dresses as a

Pilgrim. With the hat and everything."

Potentially Explosive Remark: "I don't believe anything the liberal media says."
Your Response: "You know what was definitely not liberal, turns out? The amount of Vaseline I used on my crotch before my last long run. Ouch! Guys, take it from me—you wanna really slather that stuff on."

Potentially Explosive Remark: "I voted for Trump because I'm sick of these elites running everything."
Your Response: "Oh, you wanna talk about elites—I got to meet Molly Huddle at the expo before the New York City Marathon this year and oh, my God, she is so nice."

Potentially Explosive Remark: "Trump's going to bring back American manufacturing jobs."
Your Response: "Fun fact: Did you know that New Balance still makes some running shoes here in the U.S.?"

Potentially Explosive Remark: "I heard New Balance backed Trump recently."[1]
Your Response: "HEY! WHO WANTS MORE PIE?"

---

[1] A reference to remarks a company VP made to the *Wall Street Journal* after the 2016 election.

FREE! Ready-to-Send Holiday Letter for Runners

December 5, 2016

INSTRUCTIONS: Print, circle the appropriate option(s) line by line, copy, and mail. Presto! More time for the important things. Like shopping at the Dumb Runner Store, where great gifts for runners start at just five bucks.[1]

Merry / Happy
Christmas! / Hanukkah! / Kwanzaa! / Festivus!

Dear Family / Friends / Colleagues / People I Don't Speak to the Rest of the Year,

Wow! Has it been another year already? I don't know where the time goes. Seems like only 12 months ago that I was sending my last holiday letter. Ha ha. / LOL / ☺

It's been an eventful / challenging / wonderful year, full of events / challenges / wonder—and more than a few ups and downs / surprises / open sores.

This year I traveled to Boston / Chicago / New York / _____ and saw all the sights, from the expo to the

---

[1] Visit DumbRunner.com/store!

medical tent. I really should return someday when I'm able to navigate stairs.

I had my share of injuries and setbacks this year, including problems with my feet / ITB / Achilles / back / front / knees / glutes / ex-partner / ex-partner's glutes. I am happy / sad to report that I am currently healthy / still recovering.

Please send thoughts / prayers / gift cards.

The dog is good, and as frisky as ever. / I still do not own a dog.

The kids are great—they grow up so fast! / I still do not have children.

Other than that, there is not much new to report. / We lost Mom / Dad this year.

Wishing you health and happiness in the New Year!

    Peace and Love,

_____

Man Still Waiting for "New Him" Promised Last January

December 12, 2016

For many of us, a new year means a fresh start—the chance to cast aside bad, old habits and begin anew. A time of promise, of hope, of looking forward.

But at least one local man says he's still waiting to see the "new you" that a magazine promised him last year.

"I remember the cover vividly," recalls Stan Wojciehowicz, 42, a retail analyst in Hoboken, New Jersey. "It specifically said NEW YEAR, NEW YOU, in big letters, right at the top. Then something about shaping up and slimming down and having my best year ever. And a picture of a guy without a shirt. He was ripped."

Wojciehowicz was sold.

Even though he has read the issue cover to cover several times, however, he says little has changed.

"The magazine had this recipe for Lentil and Chard Soup, so I made that and ate it," he says. "Then I did the 3 Best Stretches for Runners.

"Also, I went shopping and bought all of the 9 Foods for Injury Prevention and Health. After that I Reset My Mindset With These 5 Easy Tricks, learned 7 Secrets of Motivated People, and sprinkled lavender oil on my pillow for a better night's sleep."

Despite his efforts, Wojciehowicz says he's more or

less the same man he was 12 months ago.

"I go for runs a few times a week, and I try to eat better, but I'm still just kinda schlubby," he says, poking himself in the gut. "Still sort of bored at work. This pain in my lower back is the same.

"I'm tired."

It's not just him. Wojciehowicz's wife, Darla, agrees that there's nothing new about her husband.

"Same old Stan," she says. "Gets home from work, has dinner, plops down in front of the TV. I love the guy, don't get me wrong. But... I mean, look at him.

"I think it's not fair, what that magazine cover did," she adds. "Making promises it couldn't keep. Shame on it."

For his part, Wojciehowicz says he doesn't blame the periodical for his lack of transformation.

"I must have not done something right," he says. "Maybe I didn't make enough soup."

Whatever the reason, he's vowing to hang in there, even as the rest of us prepare to celebrate the coming of another new year.

"I don't give up very easy," says Wojciehowicz. "My New Me could appear any day now.

"I'm really looking forward to it."

Dog Who Ran Half-Marathon Accused of Cheating

January 18, 2017

A dog who ran a half-marathon last fall, becoming an internet celebrity, did not complete the entire course, says a website devoted to identifying suspicious race performances.

Samson, a 4-year-old golden retriever, made headlines in October 2016 when he appeared at the start of the Tacoma (Washington) Half Marathon and proceeded to follow the runners as the race began. Various runners reported seeing him along the course, and he crossed the finish line with the event's 1:45-hour pace group, to the delight of spectators and race officials.

That upbeat story was punctured late last week, when the website RaceCheats.com published a post accusing Samson of cutting the course and "fraudulently accepting accolades and a finisher's medal."

In its post, the website analyzed data from the official race results showing that Samson crossed the first timing mat, at the 5K mark, in 33 minutes 12 seconds and the second mat, at 10K, in 1 hour 4 minutes 41 seconds. That's an average pace of 10:25 per mile.

"Then," RaceCheats.com founder Eric Estrada said in an interview, "things get wacky."

Estrada notes that there is no record of Samson's crossing the timing mats at 15K or 20K. The next split recorded for the dog is at the finish line, which he reached in 1 hour 43 minutes 54 seconds—an average race pace of 7:56 per mile.

To make that happen, Samson would have had to run miles 6 through 13.1 at a pace of 5:41 per mile. The dog's 5K PR, according to public race results, is 22 minutes 11 seconds, which is an average pace of 7:08.

Estrada also said he was unable to find race photos of Samson between miles 6 and 12.

"Cheating is cheating, regardless of species," Estrada said. "This animal's story isn't cute. It's an outrage."

After being notified of the RaceCheats.com report, Tacoma Half Marathon race officials removed Samson's time from the official results.

Samson did not respond to calls for comment.

With Executive Order, Trump Bans Metric Race Distances

January 29, 2017

In a surprise move, President Donald Trump on Friday signed an executive order abolishing "the practice of measuring, certifying, or promoting any footrace using the metric system."

In practical terms, this spells the end for such popular road races as the 5K and 10K, as well as a virtually all track events as we know them, from the 100 meters to the 10,000m.

"The voters spoke," Trump told reporters afterward. "They voted for change, OK? They voted for putting America first, and that means using American ways to measure things. Not foreign.

"The metric system is a disaster," he continued. "Look at the countries using it. France. Germany. South America. They're failing, big league. They're falling apart. Not us. Not us. We're going back—and by the way, when I was in military school I was a tremendous athlete, everyone said it, I used to run the 440, won many awards, probably could've gone to the Olympics, decided not to—but the metric system, all these meters and kilowatts and K's and all of these things, they're going away, OK? They're going away.

"Starting now, if you're in the United States of

America, you measure your race American.

"With this executive order," he said, "we are making American races American again."

The move garnered little attention from most media outlets—understandably, given the flurry of executive orders, provocative tweets, and other drama during his first full week in office—but runners have certainly noticed.

"No more 5Ks?" asked one runner on Twitter. "WTF?"

"What are we supposed to call them now?" asked another. "3.1-milers?"

"I am prepared to fight this using every tool at my disposal," said the outspoken U.S. track star Nick Symmonds, "up to and including a defiant statement temporarily tattooed on my shoulder."

Symmonds and other opponents of the move have their work cut out for them. In his remarks to reporters following the signing of the order, President Trump underlined his intense dislike for the metric system.

"By the way," he asked rhetorically, "where did the metric system come from? Nobody knows. One day it's not there, we're using miles and feet and inches, everything is great, and then the next day, boom, metric system. All these countries use it. Why? No one knows. Nobody knows. No one asks. But suddenly all these countries are using it, and they—it's a common system. It's a common, a *global system*. And it—people are saying, many people are saying, maybe it's a plan, a U.N. plan to take over, whatever. I don't know. I have very good sources that are saying that. But I don't know. We're looking into it."

The order eliminating metric-distance races is effective February 1.

Inspired by Forrest Gump, Man Runs Across U.S., Fights in Vietnam, Gets Shot in Buttocks, Becomes Table-Tennis Champ, Buys Fleet of Shrimping Boats

February 5, 2017

When Tom Wopat told friends 13 months ago that he intended to follow in Forrest Gump's footsteps by running across the United States and then shipping himself off to fight in Vietnam and getting shot in the rear and becoming a table-tennis champ and getting into the shrimping business, they called him crazy.

But last week the 32-year-old paralegal and longtime runner made good on his vow.

"I'm tired, but happy," Wopat told reporters by phone from Bayou La Batre, Alabama, where he'd just taken ownership of the James Best Shrimp Co.—a small company with a half-dozen shrimping boats and a harborside processing facility.

"Now that I have assumed control of this shrimping fleet, my yearlong quest is complete," he said. "It's been a heck of an experience."

The experience began back in January 2016, Wopat said, when his personal life took a turn for the worse.

"I'd just gone through a bad breakup, I lost my job, and my dog died," he said. "Then I learned that my dog had only *faked* his death, and had gone to live with my ex. It was a difficult time."

Then, Wopat said, he sat down to watch TV, flipped through the channels, and stopped on *Forrest Gump*. It was, he says, "a lightbulb moment."

"Suddenly," he said, "I thought that's it. That's what I'll do. I'll just start running and I'll run and run, all the way across the country."

"And then," he continued, "I'll go fight in Vietnam, get shot, become a master at table tennis, and wind up getting into the shrimping industry. Just like Forrest."

The cross-country run, said Wopat, was the easy part.

"Managing to find a firefight in Vietnam? In this day and age? That was tough," he said. "And convincing a stranger to shoot you in the buttocks is easier said than done. Especially when he doesn't speak English."

Wopat said he was already a capable table-tennis player, so honing those skills wasn't overly challenging. The shrimp business, however, proved a taller-than-expected hurdle.

"It's not as easy as you'd think," he said. "There's all this regulation, all these codes and fees and red tape. Not to mention the whole business of getting a loan from the bank.

"I think all the bandages on my ass made the loan officer sympathetic. Which helped."

Now that he's finished what he started, what's next for Wopat?

He paused.

"I'm pretty tired," he said. "I think I'll go home."

Marlboro Announces Half-Marathon Race Series

March 7, 2017

Marlboro, the top-selling cigarette brand in the world, is getting into running.

The iconic American brand says it is launching a half-marathon franchise, officially called the Marlboro 13.1 Smokin' Fast Half Series. Events are planned in six major U.S. cities this year, with plans to increase that to a dozen or more in 2018.

The announcement came yesterday at a kickoff event in Richmond, Virginia, where the company hosted a 5K fun run and passed out free cigarettes along with steep discounts on Smokin' Fast race entries.

While a cigarette maker may seem an unlikely sponsor for a sports event, the idea isn't without precedent, says Christopher Buckley, a spokesperson for Marlboro parent company Philip Morris USA.

"Marlboro has been heavily involved in motor racing for decades," said Buckley, "having sponsored teams in Formula One, IndyCar, and Grand Prix motorcycle racing.

"Plus, remember that whole Virginia Slims tennis thing?" he said. "There was that."[1]

---

[1] There *was* that. Remember the Virginia Slims tennis tour? Crazy stuff.

As running continues to grow in popularity and tobacco sales continue to shrink, Buckley said, the Smokin' Fast Half Series seemed like a natural next step.

The tobacco giant was encouraged, he added, by the success of the Snickers Marathon and Half Marathon in Albany, Georgia.

"I mean, if a candy bar can have a marathon..." he said, with laughter that led to a coughing fit.

While Marlboro's events will be open to all, they are "designed to appeal to today's active smoker," the company said in a statement.

So while the races will offer the usual amenities—tech shirts, numerous aid stations, a finish-line festival—they will also add some unique twists, such as a finisher's medal that doubles as an ashtray and discounted rates at area hotels that accommodate smokers.

Smoking will even be encouraged during the race, according to the statement—each event will include tobacco-friendly start and finish areas, plus two Smoke Zones® along the course where competitors can pause to light up.

With entry fees starting at $100, the events will not be cheap. But, as Buckley was quick to point out, "a portion of the proceeds" will benefit the race series' charity partner, the American Lung Association.

Woman Can't Quite Place Smell She's Picking Up From Yoga Mat

April 4, 2017

A woman using the fitness center at Chicago's West Anderson Hotel can't seem to identify the smell coming from her yoga mat, Dumb Runner has learned.

"I thought it smelled a little bit off when I grabbed it," said Margot Tenenbaum, 36, an advertising executive and hotel guest. "But when I got closer I really got a good whiff.

"Wow.

"The thing is," she said, "I can't quite nail down what,

exactly, it smells like."

The mat belongs to the hotel and was chosen randomly from a pile in the fitness center, Tenenbaum said, noting that she normally travels with her own mat but left it home this time.

"I start doing my routine," she said, "and I'm thinking meat. It smells like meat. Beef, or maybe pork.

"Gradually, though, as the mat has a chance to breathe, I begin to pick up other notes, and I struggle to identify them," she said. "Molasses? Yeast? Singed hair? A hint of Axe Body Spray?"

She leaned in closer for another snort.

"Fritos?"[1]

Tenenbaum admitted she may never find precisely the right words to describe the rich olfactory tapestry found in that yoga mat, an amalgam of the odors of dozens, perhaps hundreds, of previous users.

"I'll think it over while I take a shower," she said. "A long, long shower."

---

[1] Online this was originally something...worse. I changed it at the urging of my wife. My wife is a wise person.

9 Things You Never Knew About the Boston Marathon

April 9, 2017

The 2017 Boston Marathon is just one week away. Can you believe it?

You should believe it, because it's true. On Monday, April 17, about 30,000 runners will gather in the small town of Hopkinton and await their chance to run the famed route to the finish line on Boston's Boylston Street.

It's been around since 1897, but how well do you know the Boston Marathon? Not as well as you might think, we'd wager. Did you know, for example…?

1. Its Official Name Is Not "The Boston Marathon"

The event's official name is actually the Hopkinton Tater Trot, in honor of Hopkintonians' famous love of potatoes. As the race grew and attracted international attention, however, organizers thought "Boston Marathon" lent their event more gravitas. Today, the "Tater Trot" name is used only in legal documents.

2. If You Encounter Race Director Dave McGillivray at the Start You Must Answer His "Riddles Three" Before You Can Pass

If you can't, or don't, Dave will smite you. And then taunt you, pointing and jeering, "Oh, no! You been *smote*!"

3. The Unicorn Hasn't Always Been Part of the Marathon's Logo
Early versions featured a horse wearing a fake horn. In the early 1900s the board of the Boston Athletic Association voted unanimously to replace the horn-wearing horse with the unicorn we see today.

4. The "Girls of Wellesley" Are Actually Women
Strange but true.

5. John Hancock Is a Sponsor (Shhh!)
Believe it or not, the insurance and financial services company, based in Boston, has quietly supported the race for more than 30 years. Sorry to blow your cover, guys, but we think you deserve a little recognition!

6. It Keeps Local Polish Butchers Very Busy
That's thanks to the 11,000 pounds (not a typo!) of kielbasa handed out each year at official aid stations.

7. It's the Least-Romantic Marathon in the World
No one's sure when or how this became a tradition, but during the event's 120-year history it's estimated that some 45,000 runners have broken up with their significant other at or around mile 20.5, on the course's most difficult climb. Hence its nickname: Heartbreak Hill.

8. Everyone Says a Certain Street Name Wrong
Looks easy enough, doesn't it? *Hereford?* But despite what many runners seem to think, the street that takes runners from Commonwealth Avenue to Boylston Street is pronounced "HOW-sten."

9. There's a Reason the Race Feels So Long

Few people outside the B.A.A.'s upper echelons know it, but the Boston Marathon's course is about a half-mile too long. When race officials discovered this snafu, circa 1960, they decided 26.685 miles was "close enough" and left it alone—a fitting response for a race held in Massachusetts, the "Close Enough" State.[1]

---

[1] Shout-out to the online reader who commented, apparently seriously: "Please provide USATF course measurement documentation to back up #9."

Man at Mile 2 of Boston Marathon Pretty Sure He's En Route to Huge PR

April 17, 2017

Noting his 2-mile split of 12:56—an average of 6:28 per mile—first-time Boston Marathoner Norm Peterson today told himself that he is virtually certain he has a big personal-record marathon time locked up.

Dude, I am flying, Peterson, 26, told himself as he breezed past the 2-mile marker along the course. *This feels great!*

Peterson qualified for Boston with a 3:01 marathon last fall—his current PR. That amounts to an average 6 minutes 55 seconds per mile.

At his current pace, Peterson reckoned, he is en route to a sub-2:50 finish.

The Chicago native was reportedly nervous before today's start, wondering if he could possibly run under 3 hours on the historic course. With his 2-mile split, those concerns appear to have evaporated.

Maybe I'm fitter than I realized, thought Peterson, his confidence building with each footfall. *I keep this up and maybe I could even run negative splits, do a 2:45 or something.*

This is awesome! he added to himself, grinning slightly.

As recently as a few minutes ago, Peterson was reportedly mulling whether to increase his pace a bit to "put some time in the bank."

The Newton Hills could not be reached for comment.

'Marathon' Image Laughable, Even by Stock Photo Standards

April 24, 2017

A stock photograph of an alleged marathon finish line is comically bad, Dumb Runner has learned.

The image, titled "Male Athlete Winning Marathon Race," was discovered late Sunday on a stock-image website. It depicts a small group of "runners" in what appears to be a wooded park. A white-haired man at the front of the pack smiles, arms outstretched, as he reaches a red tape, presumably representing the finish line.

Even by stock photography's already low standards, sources said, the photo is laughable for numerous reasons.

- The subjects are wearing generic "Marathon" bib numbers, which are the road racing equivalent of seeing a sitcom character ordering "a beer" and being handed something labeled "BEER."
- The bib numbers are obviously Photoshopped onto the subjects' shirts—and, in the case of the bib at far left, over the red tape.
- The photo is eerily devoid of spectators, race officials, volunteers, barriers, or any other indication of an actual race.
- The photo is also eerily devoid of perspiration.
- Everyone's hair looks fantastic.
- The woman at right is glancing at the "winner" and grinning, as if to say, *Well, you did it, you ol' son of a gun*, whereas in a real race she would be staring ahead with dead eyes and an open mouth.
- The man breaking the tape has clearly never won a marathon, and likely has never even watched someone win a marathon, which is the only way to explain his body language and expression in the photo, which are less "I am winning a marathon" and more "euphoric zombie having a stroke."
- The man breaking the tape, viewers are expected to believe, has beaten not just the young, fit-looking runners visible behind him but—based on his high bib number—at least 7,620 others in the race.
- Just the man breaking the tape, basically.

The subjects were not available for comment, as they were all attending a "business meeting" in a bright conference room, smiling at each other as the white-haired man pointed to a plain white chart showing "sales."

5 Stretches You Should Never Do

April 26, 2017

Readers, we've told you that stretching is bullshit.[1] But apparently some of you are still doing it.

This is disappointing.

However. If you insist on stretching, the least we can do is show you how to not do it unsafely.

Here are five stretches that you should absolutely avoid—despite what your high school coach might have told you!—and what you can do instead.

1. The Hanging Jerk (aka the Vertebreak)

How it's done: Standing tall and with legs straight, bend forward at the waist and reach toward the floor. When

---

[1] And we mean it.

you've bent as low as you possibly can, force your head and shoulders further downward with hard, spastic jerks.

Why you should avoid it: This move can break one or more vertebrae.

Instead, try this: Relax in a comfortable chair with a book.

2. The Lumbar Jack

How it's done: From a standing position, feet together and firmly planted, suddenly and violently whip your upper body around as far as possible while thrusting your arms outward as if you're shoving an imaginary foe or telling someone behind you, "Yo! Back off."

Why you should avoid it: It may "jack up" your lumbar nerves—hence the name—possibly leading to "some loss of function in the hips and legs" and "little or no control of bowel or bladder."

Instead, try this: Take a walk around your neighborhood.

3. The Socket Popper

How it's done: Standing straight, place one arm behind your head and reach for the opposite shoulder blade; use your free hand on the elbow to coax the arm down until you feel pressure. Continue pressing until the pressure becomes uncomfortable. Keep pressing, gritting your teeth and taking quick, shallow breaths. When you hear a loud popping sound, you'll know you're done.

Why you should avoid it: This move renders one arm useless indefinitely, and in a public setting the popping sound may be mistaken for a gunshot, causing nearby firearms enthusiasts to "return fire" in your direction.

Instead, try this: Play "hooky" from work and treat yourself to a matinee.

4. The Foot Pully-Uppy

How it's done: Standing and bracing yourself on a wall for support, bring one foot up toward your buttocks. Grab the foot and gently pull it closer until you feel pressure in your quadriceps. Hold for a few moments, then repeat with the other leg.

Why you should avoid it: This one just makes you look like a doofus.

Instead, try this: Anything else. Unless you enjoy looking like a doofus.

5. The Forehead Crunch

How it's done: Lean toward a wall, with one foot planted forward and the other behind you and forearms against the wall for support. Draw your head back and then smash it into the wall, repeatedly, to failure. Don't forget to breathe.

Why you should avoid it: Usually results in loss of consciousness, during which passersby may steal your watch.

Instead, try this: Go for a short run, starting slowly and gradually increasing the pace.

Woman Immediately Regrets Asking Date if He's Ever Run a Marathon

May 9, 2017

A woman[1] on a first date Tuesday night erred badly when she asked her companion if he had ever run a marathon. The woman realized her mistake almost immediately, sources say, but it was already too late.

The incident occurred while Mallory Keaton, 36, was dining with the man, identified as a 42-year-old sales rep

---

[1] Is this the most perfect stock photo I've ever used? Probably.

named Nick, at local restaurant Fam Li Thai.[1]

Witnesses tell Dumb Runner that the couple had seemed "happy enough" as they walked in together and were shown to a table. Over the next 20 minutes or so, they say, the couple appeared to be following the standard back-and-forth of a first date—a ritualized choreography of tentative smiles, nervous laughter, and scraps of contrived dialogue.

It was during such a dialogue that Keaton made her misstep.

Apparently prompted by photos she had seen on his social media accounts, Keaton began by asking her date about his running habits—how often he ran, for instance, and how far. Witnesses say they saw where the conversation was going, and some tried frantically to signal Keaton to change the subject.

It's impossible to know whether she didn't notice the signals or simply ignored them. Either way, Keaton went ahead, asking, "So, have you ever run a marathon?"

What followed, according to horrified onlookers, was a 16-minute monologue from her date detailing not just his most recent marathon but each of his previous three, including 5K splits, weather conditions, field size, and finishing time; plus an aside on the merits of using chip time vs. gun time and a mention of Nike's recent Breaking2 race, which itself branched off into a summation of the debate over maximalist and minimalist footwear.

Keaton tried to change the subject at least three times, sources say, but the man repeatedly steered the

---

[1] Is this the worst punny inside joke I've ever written? Definitely.

conversation back to marathons.

"Steamtown is a pretty fast course," he was heard saying as Ms. Keaton asked a server for their check.

Keaton could not be reached for comment, though sources tell Dumb Runner that her companion thought their date "went great."

The incident comes just two weeks after another local woman immediately regretted asking someone at a friend's barbecue about his Ironman tattoo.[1]

---

[1] See "Tattoos Make Runners Look Cool, Researchers Find," page 127.

"How Far Was That?" Asks Purist Who Never Runs With a Watch

May 30, 2017

A self-described "low-tech runner" who makes a point never to wear a watch asked his running partners Sunday morning how far they had just run.

"Hey, guys," Neil Peart, 37, said as he and the others wrapped up their run, "just curious—how far was that?"

"Around 10?" he ventured "Or...?"

Peart, a software engineer and part-time yoga instructor, consciously chooses never to use a GPS watch or any other kind of technology to monitor pace and distance, preferring instead to, as he frequently tells others, "run by feel and not worry about all those numbers."

Friends say he often joshes them about their own GPS watches, teasing them about their slavish devotion to data.

Reached for comment, Peart told Dumb Runner, "All those gizmos, all those numbers, they're just a distraction, you know? I'm a purist. I like to run 'naked'—no phone, nothing on my wrist, just me and my running shoes and Mother Earth. For me, it's all about the experience."

"By the way," he added, "did the guys happen to tell you how far we went this morning? Was it about 5½ , 6?"

This was not the first time Peart has engaged in such behavior, friends say, and his queries aren't limited to distance.

"He's always asking about our pace during the run, too," said one. "Like, 'Hey, what are we doing? About 8:30 pace?' It's a little annoying."

"Neil's a good guy," said another. "But you sort of wish he'd just buy a watch already."

Man Wishes He Had Time to Run

May 31, 2017

A local man has declared that he wishes he had time to run.

Jason Seaver, 45, an insurance claims adjuster and married father of two, made the announcement during a recent neighborhood block party. According to several sources who attended the gathering but aren't authorized to speak about it publicly, the subject came up as Seaver was making small talk with Rose Nylund, a neighbor and avid runner.

"Jason's been [in the neighborhood] for years, but Rose

is relatively new," said a man who overheard their conversation. "So they were sort of breaking the ice."

After a few remarks on the weather and some nearby rose bushes, he said, Seaver mentioned that he'd seen Nylund out running and asked how often and how far she ran.

"She told Jason that she runs about four times a week and she's training for her first half-marathon," the source said.

Seaver seemed impressed, he said, then told Nylund "That's really great," adding "Yeah, I wish I had time to run."

A study released last year by Nielsen found that the average American watches five hours and four minutes of television per day.[1]

At that point, sources said, the conversation returned to the weather before Seaver checked his watch and excused himself.

Reports that Seaver later told another neighbor "I wish I had time to read books" could not be independently verified.

---

[1] This is true.

"He's Friendly," Owner Assures Runner as Off-Leash Dog Pierces Carotid Artery

June 13, 2017

A local runner says he was relieved yesterday to learn that the dog who attacked him was friendly.

Richard Van Dyke, 34, was running alone on the Poppins Park jogging path around 7 a.m. Tuesday, he said, when he first noticed something out of the corner of his eye. That something turned out to be Bert, a 4-year-old mixed breed bolting, off-leash, away from his owner.

"He was a blur," Van Dyke recalled from his bed at St. Mary's Hospital. "Like a cruise missile. Before I knew it, this dog was airborne and headed right for my throat.

"You can imagine my relief," he said, "when the dog's owner shouted to me that he was harmless."

By the time passersby were able to separate the pup from Van Dyke—using their feet and, in one case, a bicycle pump—Bert had managed to locate and puncture Van Dyke's right carotid artery.

"He likes you!" said the dog's owner, who by then had reached the runner and the onlookers trying to stanch the flow of blood.

The dog then turned on several bystanders, clawing at one woman's bare legs and knocking over two small children.

"He's 4 but he still acts like a puppy," his owner said, laughing.

"Bert!" he added. "Down."

Doctors say Van Dyke is expected to make a full recovery.

"It's unfortunate that [the dog's] enthusiasm got away from him and sent me to the E.R.," said Van Dyke. "But the greater tragedy would have been seeing such a beautiful creature in the great outdoors restrained by a leash.

"Dogs were meant to be free," he added, before calling a nurse for morphine.

Bert, who apparently had tracked Van Dyke by scent, was last seen barreling into the hospital's lobby, knocking over an empty wheelchair before caroming into the cafeteria.

Hospital staff and visitors reportedly were alarmed until Bert's owner shuffled in moments later with a leash draped around his neck and announced, "Don't worry, he's OK."

Lawyer for Family of Slain Raccoon Disputes Runner's Claim of Self-Defense

June 16, 2017

When a Maine runner named Rachel Borch headed to the woods for a trail run recently, she wasn't expecting to encounter a raccoon—much less an aggressive, rabid one.

That is exactly what happened, though, she said. And the ensuing battle—which ended with a terrified Borch drowning the animal in a puddle with her bare hands[1]—

---

[1] Another weird-but-true story. By the way: I don't mean to brag, but I totally created that photo illustration all by myself. From six photos! (Seriously.)

soon went viral, shared among runners and non-runners alike.

Today an already unusual story took a strange turn as an attorney representing the dead raccoon's family announced plans for a wrongful-death lawsuit.

"For humans, apparently, this tragic story is somehow funny," William Burrows, a prominent woodland lawyer, told a gaggle of reporters this morning near the scene of the incident. "For the family and loved ones of Stewart, however, this is no laughing matter. This is a case of cold-blooded murder, plain and simple."

Stewart is the name of the deceased raccoon.

"Compounding this tragedy," Burrows continued, adjusting his tiny eyeglasses, "is the way the media have presented the so-called facts, taking Ms. Borch at her word without even the pretense of hearing the other side."

In Borch's telling, the incident was a simple matter of self-defense. From a story in the *Bangor Daily News*:

In the midst of appreciating the weather and scenery, she looked ahead and noticed a raccoon obstructing the narrow footpath, baring its tiny teeth.

Suddenly, it began "bounding" toward her, Borch recalled. ...

"I knew instantly it had to be rabid," said Borch. ...

What felt like a split second later, the furry animal was at her feet. Borch said she was "dancing around it," trying to figure out what to do.

"Imagine the Tasmanian Devil," she said. "It was terrifying."

Burrows disputes that claim, saying that Stewart had no history of violence or rabies—and, as a father of five, had plenty to live for.

"Perhaps you've heard the species referred to as the 'common raccoon,'" Burrows said. "Well, there was nothing common about Stewart. He was a fine animal. A loving husband. A doting father. A good forager. And now he's gone. Forever."

Burrows said he intends to file the lawsuit as early as Monday. He did not specify the damages being sought.

Borch was unavailable for comment; a squirrel reporter approaching the Borch home was shooed away with a broom.

7 Essential Tips for Running the Western States 100

June 20, 2017

This weekend, hundreds of hard-core ultra runners will tackle Western States—"one of the ultimate endurance tests in the world," according to the event's website.

Officially known as the Western States 100-Mile Endurance Run—or "Badwater," for short—the event actually takes competitors 100.2 miles from its start in California's Squaw Valley to the finish line in Auburn.

If you'll be among them, here are some tips that will help to ensure a fun, safe, and successful race.

1. Be Prepared
Remember, Western States isn't just any marathon—it's a 100-mile marathon! Before "toeing the line," you should have at least one long run of 20 miles under your belt. Remember, too, that much of the challenge is mental. So also prepare your mind somehow.

2. Get There Early
You'll want to arrive at least an hour before the start to snag a good parking spot—and to register, if you didn't do so online. Make checks payable to "Western States" or "Western States 100" or "Badwater."

If you can pull it off, you might even consider arriving

a full *day* early. That way you can run the course and familiarize yourself with it before race day.

3. Line Up Where You Belong
Western States may be longer than a 5K marathon,[1] but many of the same rules apply. For instance: If you're running with a jogging stroller,[2] start at the back of the pack for safety's sake.

4. Use Fresh Shoes
One hundred miles is a long way to run, so you'll want shoes that are as new as possible. We recommend using a pair straight from the box.

5. Pass Politely
"Please be courteous to hikers, other runners, and horsemen" sharing the trail, says the event's website. This means pausing, if necessary, to let faster runners pass and announcing your own intention to overtake a hiker or runner.

Also from the website: "Runners should never pass a horse from behind without first notifying the rider." Tradition dictates that the first notification be in writing, though follow-ups may be verbal.

If the horse is riderless and wearing a bib number, then he is a fellow competitor. In that case, a clap on the rump and a "good job!" is in order.

---

[1] See page 39.

[2] See page 129.

6. Don't Sign Anything After Mile 20

As the race wears on, you'll be extremely fatigued and struggling to think clearly—i.e., lacking in judgment. If a strange man or woman appears before you on the trail, asking for your "John Hancock" on something, ignore the request—even if the stranger is dressed well, assures you that the document is just boilerplate, etc.—and report him or her at the next aid station.

7. Be Sure to Say Hi to Race Mascot Besty McWesty

Western States is so named because of its longtime title sponsor, Best Western Hotels & Resorts.[1] They're also the folks behind the event's beloved mascot, Besty McWesty[2]. If you spot Besty on the course, say hello and rub his nose for good luck. Western States may be tough—but it should be fun, too!

---

[1] It's not.

[2] Besty McWesty does not exist. But he should. If you agree, contact Best Western Hotels & Resorts, 6201 N. 24th Parkway, Phoenix, AZ 85016.

Poor Bastard Has No Idea He's Running All Wrong

June 25, 2017

Local runners say they're taking pity on a man they've spotted running around town in recent weeks, noting that the poor bastard obviously has no clue what he's doing.

"No one's sure who he is," said Alex Rogan, 33, one of a small group of serious runners who have noticed the mystery man. "But, wow… this guy is clearly uninformed."

"He's a total heel-striker," said Maggie Gordon, 41, another member of the group. "For starters."

"Also, his fists are clenched way too tight," added Jack Blake, 29. "And there's no way his cadence is anywhere near 180."

"More like 118!" said Gordon, to laughter.

To the untrained eye, the man in question appears loose and comfortable. Indeed, other onlookers who have seen him say he seems "content" and even happy during his sporadic weeknight jaunts.

The runners observing him, however, say they see beyond such superficialities and can rattle off any number of missteps, omissions, and blunders. Among them:

• An apparent lack of hydration and fuel. "He's never carrying any fuel," said Gordon. "Or hydration. Nada."

• Cotton socks. "What's he on?" asked Blake. "A suicide mission?"

- No warmup. "I saw him begin a run once," said Rogan. "I didn't expect him to perform all five essential prerun dynamic stretches. But this dude didn't even do static stretches. He just started running. Cold!"

The trio, who say they are self-taught running experts thanks to social media and running websites, also speculate that the man never foam rolls, seldom if ever strengthens his core, likely needs new running shoes, and, if pressed, couldn't name even one postrun eating mistake that he's probably making, much less all nine of them.

"I'd guess he isn't even on Strava," Blake said.

The very worst part, all three agreed, was that the man probably thought he was "just fine."

"I guess ignorance really is bliss," said Gordon.

"Sad," added Blake.

The mystery runner was last seen humming to himself as he paused at a water fountain before continuing on his way.

"That's Why I Carry," Gun-Loving Runner Replies to Increasing Number of Stories

June 27, 2017

Francis Macomber wants you to know he has a gun and is ready to use it—even while he's out getting his exercise.

A firearms enthusiast and runner, the 31-year-old Macomber has become much more vocal on that subject in recent months, friends say—particularly online, where he has been commenting "That's why I carry" on an increasing number and variety of posts.

The word *carry* is popular among those who enjoy moving about in public with loaded guns on their person.

"The first time I saw that comment from Frank, I didn't really give it much thought," said Robert Wilson, a longtime friend and fellow runner. "He shared an article, I think, about some lady who'd fought off an attacker during a run. His only remark was, 'This is why I carry.'"

Soon after, his friends say, that phrase—or variations on it—began popping up more and more frequently in Macomber's comments.

"That was right around the same time he stopped using the word *gun*," said Wilson, "and starting saying *weapon* instead. Things got a little weird."

Macomber's Facebook and Twitter accounts reflect that shift.

In response to a story about a man who had been chased by a dog during a run through a residential neighborhood:

"That's why I carry. Your dog comes at me, I will not hesitate to put a bullet in its brain."

To a hiker's anecdote about encountering a snake of indeterminate species on a trail:

"And that is why I carry, my friend."

To a story about a South African ultra runner "robbed of his trainers and watch" in Johannesburg:

"That's why I carry. Want my shoes, thug? I got a little surprise for you, it's called a .380."

To a story about violence at a political rally in the South:

"This is why I carry. You never know."

And, mystifyingly, to a story about the Asian carp, an aggressively invasive species recently discovered 9 miles from Lake Michigan:

"This is why I carry. I don't want to unholster and use my

weapon, but if I have to I absolutely will."

His friends confess that Macomber's behavior has them concerned for his well-being—and their own.

"A few days ago, I posted a photo of this amazing salad I'd made myself, with grilled shrimp," said a woman who gave her name only as Margot. "Everyone was 'liking' it and leaving 'nom nom' comments. Then Frank shows up and says, 'This is why I carry.'"

"Frank is a good guy, but he's always been a bit...highstrung," said Wilson. "To be honest, we were all a little nervous when he bought a handgun."

"More so when he started running with it," added Margot. "I was like, *Dude. What the f***.*"

Reached for comment via Facebook, Macomber responded with a meme likening guns to fire extinguishers.

"That's why I carry," he wrote.

Spectator Admits She Not Really Sure Marathoners Got This

July 9, 2017

A woman watching a marathon Sunday confessed that—contrary to her shouts of encouragement—she was not convinced that every runner she cheered had, in fact, got this.

Angie Merkel, 49, made the admission after being questioned by a reporter.

"You're right," she said. "I don't know who's truly got this and who doesn't. I guess I've been using the phrase pretty indiscriminately."

Merkel, whose sister was running the race, estimates that she shouted "You got this!" at 75 to 100 runners during the hour or so she had been standing along mile 14 of the race route—despite knowing "absolutely nothing" about any of the athletes streaming past her.

"I may have gotten out a bit over my skis there," Merkel said. "Truth be told, I have no idea how these runners will fare between here and the finish. Maybe some of them didn't train properly. Maybe others started way too fast, or are hurt or just having an off day.

"Has each and every one of them got this?" she asked. "Not likely."

In hindsight, she said, "I did not choose my words as carefully as I might have."

Imagining a hypothetical runner who clearly doesn't got this, and knows it, Merkel said that her cheer may sound less like words of encouragement and more like a cruel, ironic taunt.

"He knows he doesn't got this," she said. "He knows it's no secret that he doesn't got this. For me to tell him, then, that he *has* got this is just twisting the knife, isn't it?"

A struggling runner approached, and Merkel paused to cheer him on as he stopped to vomit.

"You look great!" she shouted.

Catcalling Motorist Rear-Ends Full Septic Truck, According to Runner's Fantasy

July 17, 2017

Moments after harassing a small group of local runners, a motorist slammed into the back of a full septic truck, according to one runner's fantasy.

The collision sent 4,500 gallons of raw human sewage pouring into the man's vehicle, a late-model convertible with the top down. Because he was screaming in terror, the runner's fantasy reported, much of the waste found its way into his mouth.

It was a stunning turn of events for the unnamed man, who had just passed the runners, three area women who often run together. As he drove by, the man slowed to leer at the runners, shouting, "Oh, yeah" and "Love those ******s, ladies, mmmm" among other lascivious remarks.

The truck, which was stopped just around a bend in the road, had just filled its tank at a local Mexican food festival, according to the fantasy. The fantasy also reported that the man in the convertible had "floored it" after making his remarks to the runners, so was traveling at a high rate of speed as he rounded the curve and met the truck blocking his way.

With no time to react, the runner imagined, the man rammed the back of the truck at speed, sending the contents of its full tank—which were warm, thanks to the hot, sunny weather—into the man's open car "like a tsunami of urine and feces."

The man's car had just been washed, waxed, and detailed, the runner's fantasy said, at a car wash where the man berated two employees for unevenly applying leather conditioner to his car's seats and failed to tip any of the workers.

According to the runner's fantasy, the motorist was unavailable for comment, because of the violent illness he'd contracted after swallowing at least half a gallon of the septic truck's contents.

Local Runner Hopes to Pass Love of Obsessively Recording and Tracking Data Along to Children

July 18, 2017

For Richard Marin, running is more than a way to keep fit and healthy—it's also a chance to model positive behavior for his two young children.

"As a dad, I know my kids look up to me," said Marin, 31, a father to Tommy, 4, and Natasha, 5 months, "and I know they pay attention more to what grown-ups do than to what we say."

That's why, Marin said, he "leads by example" to impart to his children the importance of compulsively recording the details of every run via a variety of gadgets and apps, using every conceivable metric, and then sorting and charting the data over time.

"[As a nation] we're getting less and less healthy, and more and more obese," he said. "I want my kids to buck those trends. I want them to grow up in a home where a pathological need to measure and track the data of your workouts is the norm."

On a recent afternoon in his comfortable suburban home, Marin, a software engineer and veteran of five marathons, showed a reporter what he meant by that.

"See, Daddy is uploading his workout," he said as he pecked away at a laptop computer while balancing 5-month-old Natasha on one knee. "Can you say 'Garmin Connect'?"

As he told his daughter about heart-rate zones, course segments, and the difference between Fitbit Activity Minutes and Garmin Intensity Minutes, Marin noticed his son enter the room.

"Hey, buddy, what's up?" he said. "We're just about to examine the elevation profile of my runs so far this week and see how they compare to the same period of time last year, graphed against my weight and average pace, if you want to join us."

Tommy, on his way outside to play, did not.

"He loves this stuff," said Marin, laughing. "As soon as he was old enough to walk, Tommy had his own Fitbit, smart socks, and Strava account."

As Natasha chewed on a heart-rate monitor chest strap, Marin reached down to plug one of his several GPS watches into a wall outlet.

"Too many kids miss out on this," he said. "And that's a shame."

11 Terrible[1] Jokes for Runners

July 23, 2017

Q: What's a runner's favorite Hungarian dish?
A: GU-lash.

Q: What did the coach say after watching his runner complete a mile at marathon pace?
A: "I'm sorry—could you repeat that?"

Knock, knock.
Who's there?
Beak.
Beak who?
Not yet—but I'll make it to Boston one of these years.[2]

A rabbi, a priest, and an atheist walk into a bar. The bartender says, "What'll it be, fellas?" All three of them reply, "Just water. We have a marathon tomorrow."

Q: What's the difference between large parties at restaurants and runners?
A: Large parties at restaurants split their checks; runners check their splits.

---

[1] No, really. They're bad.

[2] "Beak who," "BQ"... Get it? No?

Knock, knock.
Who's there?
Orange.
Orange who?
Orange you glad I didn't show you my toenails?

Q: What do you call a runner who's wearing earbuds?
A:
Q: I *said*, What do you call a runner who's wearing earbuds?
A:

Q: Why did the runner cross the road?
A: Because that's where the less-crowded aid station was.

Knock, knock.
Who's there?
Eyesore.
Eyesore who?
Eyesore from my long run—can we take the elevator?

Did you hear about the ultra runners who lived in different cities? They had a long-distance relationship.

Knock, knock.
Who's there?
Hydrate.
Hydrate who?
Hydrate you a 9 out of 10, at least!

Tattoos Make Runners Look Cool, Researchers Find

July 30, 2017

A new study has confirmed what many have long suspected: Tattoos make runners look cool.[1]

The study, from researchers at the University of California, Davis, appears in the current issue of *The American Journal of Dermatological Embellishment*.

"Whether it's something as simple as a Chinese symbol or line of text, or as complex as an elaborate 'sleeve,' getting some ink is absolutely a way for runners to up their coolness quotient," said lead researcher Hervé Villechaize, Ph.D.

To conduct their study, Villechaize and his colleagues analyzed 32 subjects—18 men and 14 women between 19 and 64 years old. Half of the subjects had at least one tattoo, half had none. All subjects were regular runners, ranging from a self-described "jogger" to a two-time Olympic Marathon Trials qualifier.

The researchers then observed each subject as he or she ran on a treadmill for 20 minutes, varying the speed and incline at random intervals. They also watched as each subject cooled down afterward, stretched, drank from a water bottle, and stood peering at the horizon in a very

---

[1] I have five. You do the math.

serious way.

In each scenario, they reported, "the ones with tattoos just looked cooler."

Interestingly, the researchers said, temporary tattoos did not have the same effect. They aren't sure why, though they speculate the reason may be that most temporary cartoons are designed with children in mind and therefore look silly.

The researchers did find one exception to the rule.

"An Ironman logo tattoo actually *decreases* a runner's coolness quotient by at least 50%," the study declares. "We therefore strongly advise runners to avoid getting one. Or, if they already have one, to consider having it removed."

What does all this mean for the average, middle-of-the-pack runner? Would Villechaize recommend that every runner get one or more tattoos?

"Without question," he said. "We don't see a downside."

Woman Pretty Sure 5K's Ban on Strollers Doesn't Apply to Her

August 1, 2017

Explaining that she is very careful and will "stay out of people's way," a local mom said she was sure an upcoming 5K's ban on strollers did not apply to her.

"Yeah, they say 'No dogs, no strollers,' but, you know," said Bonnie Parker, 32. "It'll be fine."

The race in question, the Middletown Parks Joggest August 5K, explicitly forbids strollers of any kind, citing "the potential for injuries to participants, including children." The prohibition is spelled out on the event website's Rules and Regulations page, on the home page of the official website, and in the race packet accompanying each participant's bib number.

Parker, who has a 19-month-old son, said she regularly runs with her child in a jogging stroller.

"We've run together a bunch," she said. "I can see why [the organizers] would say 'no strollers,' but in our case, it's all good.

"We won't start in the front," she explained. "And I'll turn my tunes down to a safe level."

The 5K also forbids MP3 players, headphones, and earbuds.

Asked for comment, the event's organizers directed a reporter to the website's Rules and Regulations page and reiterated that the exclusion of strollers helps to ensure the safety of all—adults as well as children. They also said the event is required to prohibit things like strollers, skates, and animals by the event's insurance provider.

Parker brushed aside such concerns.

"They have to say that stuff," she said. "Yada yada yada, legal mumbo jumbo.

"It'll be fine," she said, again.

Witnesses at the 5K's packet pickup location later reported that Parker left her SUV in a handicap parking space, despite having no permit or placard, explaining to onlookers that she "would only be a few minutes."

Wow! Check Out These 5 Celebs Who Won't Be Running the 2017 NYC Marathon

August 13, 2017

On November 5, an estimated 50,000 runners will compete in the 2017 New York City Marathon—and we know five celebrities who won't be among them!

Keep reading, and prepare to be floored!

Harrison Ford

The original Indy rock star hates snakes and Nazis and... running? We can't say for sure, but he surely will not be running NYC this November! Maybe instead he'll fly one of his planes somewhere—Solo!

Julia Louis-Dreyfus

She's the Veep of our hearts, and we'd pay good money to see what sort of funky dance she might perform at the finish line of the New York City Marathon—but it looks like that won't happen this year, because she won't be running! Not that there's anything wrong with that!

Danny DeVito

This film fave won't be running the New York City Marathon! Will he take a Taxi with Other People's Money to cheer on runners at the finish line? We wouldn't put it past this Shorty! Hey, Be Cool—it's a Term of Endearment!

Katie Couric
Yahoo! America's Sweetheart has a killer journalistic résumé behind that dazzling smile! Will she be running this year's New York City Marathon? We won't make you wait 60 Minutes for the answer—it's no!

George Strait
Nope!

Woman Who Runs "to Escape the News" Hasn't Stopped Since Last Wednesday

August 15, 2017

For Leia Fisher, running has always been a way to tune out what she calls "all the crazy in the world," at least temporarily.

"Running is how I cope with difficult stuff," she said in a recent interview as she ran through her middle-class neighborhood in Sacramento, California. "It's my therapy."

In today's 24/7 news cycle, she said, it's also the only time she's able "to completely escape the news" and forget, for a while, things like war, natural disasters, political tension, and other unpleasant realities.

Given the events of the past week or so, this has created a problem: Fisher has now been running nonstop since last Wednesday afternoon.

"I headed out for a run around 2 p.m. that day," she said, "after reading about the Guam thing."

Fisher was referring to threats by North Korea to launch nuclear-armed missiles at the U.S. territory of Guam, heightening an already-tense war of words between that nation's leadership and U.S. President Donald Trump.

"This was the day after the 'fire and fury' remarks," she said, "and I was just, like, you know what? F*** this. I'm going for a run."

She returned about 40 minutes later, she said, and "after one look at Twitter…turned right around and got back to running."

Seven days later, she's still at it—and exhausted. Fisher estimates she's run approximately 540 miles since she started. (Her Garmin's battery died sometime Saturday.) And for the 31-year-old marketing consultant, there's no end in sight.

"On Friday, I paused and it looked like things were back to normal," she said. "Relatively speaking, at least. Just as I'm about to grab a drink and collapse on the couch, what comes on the TV? Charlottesville.

"Back out I went."

Fisher said her pace has slowed, but she's determined to keep going as long as it takes to outlast a seemingly never-ending stream of awful news.

"I'm utterly wiped out," she said, "exhausted, drained, near tears, my feet are bloody and raw.

"Still," she added, "it beats watching the news."

Runners, Here Is Your Solar Eclipse FAQ

August 20, 2017

As media-savvy citizens, you probably know a lot by now about Monday's total solar eclipse—the first seen in the continental U.S. since 1979. As runners, however, you are probably desperate for answers to some pressing runner-specific questions.

We are here to answer those questions.

Q: How will the eclipse affect my form?
A: For a brief period, it will make it darker than usual.

I have a speed workout scheduled during the eclipse. Should I postpone it?
Yes, just to be safe.

What if I do it on the treadmill?
Oh. Yeah, that should be fine.

How should I fuel for the eclipse?
Duh:

MoonPie... What a time to be alive![1]
You said it.

How should I hydrate for the eclipse?
For the best results, we recommend using fluids.

Which stretches should I avoid during a solar eclipse?
The same ones you should avoid every other day.[2]

Can I look directly at the sun?
No.

What if I'm using my Name Brand Running Eyewear™?
You mean sunglasses?

No. These cost $140, so they're called "eyewear."
They're sunglasses, and the answer is no.

I'm really into planking lately, and as a result my core is super strong.
That's terrific, but you still shouldn't look directly at the sun.

Just sake of argument here, but what would happen to my eyes, theoretically, if I did look directly at the sun?
You know what? They're your eyes. Do whatever you want.

---

[1] *Simpsons* reference!

[2] See page 94.

Is there a store somewhere called Eclipse Running?
Yes—in Reno, Nevada. It was opened in 1994 by a guy named Chuck, whose photo is on the store's website. Chuck looks like a guy we'd like to have a beer with.

Can I look directly at Chuck?
Yes.

In a CNN.com article, does J. Kelly Beatty, senior editor of *Sky & Telescope*, compare viewing a total solar eclipse to "being on your wedding night"?
He does.[1]

Uhh... What does J. Kelly Beatty do during these events, exactly?
That is a question for J. Kelly Beatty.

I've heard that during the eclipse the temperature may fall, the wind may go still, and certain animals may behave as if to say, "Hey, what the f* just happened?" True?**
There is no scientific evidence to support the notion that animals swear, even to themselves. Also, these questions are getting less and less runner-specific.

I run with some friends who believe that a solar eclipse is the sun being slowly devoured by the decapitated head of a Hindu demon. What's the best way to address this?
Well, that's what some believe; scientists believe that the

---

[1] Yep. He does.

complex interplay of astronomical geometry periodically aligns the sun, Earth, and moon so that the moon completely obscures the light of the sun for a period of time.

As usual, the truth probably lies somewhere in the "murky middle." Mollify your friends with some MoonPies and change the subject.

Rejected Marriage Proposal at Mile 13 Makes Second Half of Marathon Awkward

August 22, 2017

Norville Rogers had big plans for Sunday's Crystal Cove (California) Marathon.

Unbeknownst to Daphne Blake, his girlfriend of 18 months, tucked away in the 27-year-old's waist pack was a diamond engagement ring. At mile 13.1, the halfway point, Rogers would slow to a walk, kneel before Blake, and ask for her hand in marriage.

That's exactly what he did—and everything went according to plan, until Blake said "no."

"I think her exact words were '*God* no,'" said Hanna Barbera, 33, a spectator who watched the bungled proposal as it happened. "Like, for emphasis."

After an uncomfortable silence, witnesses said, the two rejoined the race.

"It was super awkward," Barbera said.

Friends and family gathered at the halfway point, waiting with cell phone cameras and sparkling apple juice, eventually drank their juice and dispersed.

Despite the painful rejection, according to timing data, Rogers and Blake ran together for the duration of the race.

"It was a little weird," Rogers said, "but, you know, we had the same time goal and we were wearing the same pace bands."

Asked how their relationship might change after this, Rogers sighed.

"I don't know," he said. "I guess I seriously misjudged us, and where we are right now.

"I wonder if we're still on for that turkey trot."[1]

---

[1] They aren't.

"You Got This," Disembodied Head of Jerry Orbach Tells Runner in Marathon's Final Miles

September 5, 2017

A local man in the closing miles of a marathon this weekend got some encouragement from an unlikely source—the giant, ghostly head of the late actor Jerry Orbach.

"Hey, listen, you got this," the gauzy visage told Richard Wolf, 46, with Orbach's trademark sardonic delivery. "One foot in front of the other."

Orbach, perhaps best known as Detective Lennie Briscoe in TV's long-running *Law & Order*, died in 2004.

The head materialized somewhere between miles 23 and 24 of the Topeka (Kansas) Marathon. That was about 20 minutes after Wolf had "hit the wall, pretty hard," according to witnesses, and had slowed to a crawl, blinking hard and bumping into the runners streaming past him.

"Snap out of it!" the head growled as Wolf stopped abruptly and stared down at his shoes. "Two miles to go."

It worked. Wolf went on to finish the race, staggering across the line in 4:49, where he was met by a cheering section that included Abraham Lincoln, the 1976 Cincinnati Reds, and Edward the cat, a childhood pet.

"You saw it, right?" Wolf asked a large tank of oxygen minutes later, in the medical tent. "So beautiful. Jerry F***ing Orbach, man."

For a brief moment, the enormous floating head reappeared at the foot of Wolf's cot.

"Ouch," it said. "Looks more like the wall hit *you*."

Witnesses say that Wolf responded by laughing and shouting "DUN-DUN," prompting nearby medical staff to sedate him.

The ethereal, semitranslucent head could not be summoned for comment.

Selfish Jerk to Run Marathon Just for Himself

September 10, 2017

This fall, tens of thousands of runners will line up at marathon starting lines across the nation. They'll run for a multitude of charitable causes, raising money and awareness for everything from MS to veterans' care to breast cancer.

Not Andrew Griffith.

Griffith, a 34-year-old veterinary technician from Greensboro, North Carolina, is registered for the Mount Airy Marathon next month. And when he toes the line on race morning, Dumb Runner has learned, he'll be running for one person and one person alone: Andrew Griffith.

Contacted for comment, Griffith confirmed that he will not be raising funds for disease prevention and research; disadvantaged children; abandoned or abused animals; environmental protection; homelessness; adult literacy; hunger relief; kidney research; disaster aid; hospice providers; clean water; suicide prevention; elder care; or autism awareness.

"I'm just doing the marathon," Griffith said, adding that he volunteers twice a month at a nearby food bank and recently donated $100 for hurricane relief efforts. "I'm hoping to run sub-3:20."

Runners reacted to the news with revulsion and

disbelief.

"Wow," said George Lindsey, a three-time marathon finisher who has run for a variety of cancer charities. "So this guy is *for* cancer, then?"

Hope Summers, a volunteer running coach for Team Patriot Paws, which raises money for wounded K9 veterans, expressed similar sentiments.

"Through Team Patriot Paws, our marathoners have raised over $86,000 for brave military dogs who have been wounded in action," she said. "But I guess that wouldn't mean anything to [Griffith)].

"Running a marathon just for...What? Your own personal glory?" she added. "What a selfish a******."

Notified of Griffith's intentions, officials with the Mount Airy (North Carolina) Marathon issued the following statement on the event's Facebook page:

We were saddened to learn of a registrant who plans to run (the marathon) next month despite having no ties to a charity or cause of any kind. As proud supporters of awareness, this concerns us deeply.

We are in the process of contacting this individual to determine next steps.

Runners Marvel at Strange Symbols Painted on City Streets

September 12, 2017

Runners in Philadelphia say they're mystified by odd pictographs painted on streets throughout the city.

The symbols, always in white, consist of two circles and a mushroom-like icon loosely joined with a collection of angular shapes. Because the symbols appear directly in the narrow lanes favored by runners, many locals have speculated that they are some sort of message directed at them.

"It depends on how you look at it," said Thomas Yorke, 29, one such runner. "From one angle, it almost looks like a sort of face, with two eyes and a little puckered mouth and a really messed-up nose.

"But why would someone take the time to paint that on a public street?"

Others wonder whether the indecipherable glyphs are the work of a guerrilla artist.

"I heard Banksy is behind it," said Jon Greenwood, 44, another regular runner, referring to the anonymous street artist and activist based in the United Kingdom. "Which makes sense. To me, it's obviously a political statement. I mean, look at it."

For now, the provenance of the artwork remains a mystery. One recent afternoon a small group of runners stood around one such symbol as cyclists streamed around them, and no one knew quite what to make of the puzzle.

"Obviously this meant something to whoever painted it," said one. "But what?"

New "Cholera Caper" Mud Run Series Will Test Athletes' Stamina, Bowels

September 19, 2017

A new adventure race series is promising competitors the usual mud, obstacles, and camaraderie but with "an exciting new twist"—the threat of contracting cholera, an acute, diarrheal illness.

The Cholera Caper series is the brainchild of Florentino Ariza, a longtime runner and event organizer. In an interview with Dumb Runner, Ariza said he got the idea while doing an obstacle race in his native South America.

"I had paid good money to do this event," he said, "and I realized about halfway through that I was bored.

"It was, like, *OK, here's the wooden wall. Here's the barbed wire. Ooh, look out—a fire pit!*" he said, in mock horror. "Then I noticed another runner, crawling next to me, get a mouthful of mud. And it hit me. Cholera. Now that would make things interesting."

The Centers for Disease Control and Prevention describes cholera this way:

The infection is often mild or without symptoms, but can sometimes be severe. Approximately one in 10 (5–10%) infected persons will have severe disease characterized by profuse watery diarrhea, vomiting, and leg cramps. In these people, rapid loss of body fluids leads to dehydration and shock. Without treatment, death can occur within hours.

In other words, Ariza explained, physical barriers and challenges are one thing; the possibility of getting hit with violent diarrhea—and, yes, even death, he said—took things to a whole new level. Thus was Cholera Caper born.

Ariza said he and his team lace "some" of the water and mud obstacles on their race courses—only they know which ones—with *Vibrio cholerae*, the intestines-attacking bacterium responsible for cholera. And then they wait.

"So you swallow some muddy water during our event," he said. "Uh oh! Will you get cholera at some point over the next few hours? The next day? The day after that? Maybe you will. Maybe you won't.

"You just don't know," he said. "And that thrill, the not knowing, is what makes our event unique."

The idea already appears to be taking off. Registration for the first Cholera Caper event, to be held in San Francisco, sold out within hours of opening, despite its $150 price tag.

"I'm super pumped," said Alfred Knopf, 28, a book designer who was among the first to sign up. "Finishing the race will be cool, of course. But not knowing whether I'll be racked hours or days later with violent diarrhea and vomiting? That will be the real rush.

"Plus," he said, "race photos are free."

Local Runner Lets Age Slow Him Down

September 26, 2017

At an age when most of his peers are slowing down and becoming less active, one local runner is doing that as well.

Ralph Furley turns 78 next week and he says that, for him, age is a barrier.

"I ran competitively back in school," said Furley during a recent interview in his modest two-story home. "Gave it up for a while, but got back into it in my 30s. I ran some marathons here and there, but mostly just did it for enjoyment and to stay in shape."

In recent years, however, injuries and illnesses have taken a toll.

"I've always tried to take care of myself," Furley said, "but let's face it. You can only do so much. Eventually the body just starts to give out on you."

Experts said Furley is correct. As we age, bones and muscles weaken, the immune system is less able to stave off infection and illness, and incontinence becomes more common.

"It makes perfect sense that age would slow down a near-octogenarian," said Janet Wood, Ph.D., director of the Ritter Institute for Aging. "Even one who had been an avid runner for decades."

People who know Furley confirmed that age is more

than just a number for the retired mechanical engineer, who earlier this year had a hip replacement.

"Ralph mostly just sits around watching TV and reading," said Helen Roper, a longtime friend. "Getting older has definitely limited what he can do physically. For him, age is a real constraint."

The last time Furley laced up his running shoes, he said, was about six months ago.

"I got about three blocks before my sciatica flared up," he said, "and I thought, *Jeez, f*** this*."

Furley said he hopes to serve as a role model for others, showing them that it's OK not to be an inspiration to others, adding that he also has no plans to skydive on his 80th birthday, in case anybody was wondering.

"I'm tired," he said. "Tired and old."

Churchgoer Delayed by Marathon Unleashes String of Curse Words

October 3, 2017

A local man on his way to church was incensed[1] Sunday morning to find his usual route blocked by a stream of marathon runners.

Winston Smith, 51, was on his way to the 9 a.m. service at Our Ministry of Peace—about a 3-mile drive from his home—when he encountered barriers and a police officer holding traffic at an intersection.

"Oh what the ****!" Smith shouted from his car. "What the **** is this?"

Smith's vehicle was among a half-dozen or so waiting to cross the road. Witnesses said that while none of the motorists seemed happy about the delay, Smith seemed particularly irate.

Lowering his window, the devout churchgoer and father of two made his frustration known.

"Hey! ***holes!" he said. "Some of us have places to go!"

"This is bull****," he added, gesturing at the passing

---

[1] Kudos to my copy editor, the ever-capable Patty Gloeckler, for recognizing this as a pun even though I originally did not.

runners. "You have got to be ****ing kidding me."

After a few minutes of waiting, witnesses said, a gap in the field appeared and race volunteers pulled the barriers aside as the police officer waved traffic through the intersection.

"About ****ing time," Smith muttered as he pulled ahead, glaring at volunteers and spectators.

"Hey," he added, "next time try running your little race on a ****ing trail or something."

It was unclear whether Smith made it to church on time.

Woman in Porta Potty Sure Taking Her Sweet-Ass Time

October 15, 2017

A woman inside a portable toilet at a local race sure is taking her sweet-ass time, Dumb Runner has learned.

"She's been in there at least five minutes," said Clarice Starling, a runner who is currently third in line for the toilet in question. "I mean, that might not sound like a lot, but you try standing here and counting that out. Five. Solid. Minutes. While the rest of us are here waiting."

Starling paused to stare, unblinking, at the color-coded dial above the handle on the porta potty door. The dial, showing red, did not move.

"Oh, my God," she added.

As five minutes ticked over into six, the rest of the line grew restless.

"What is she doing in there?" asked Jack Crawford, a fellow competitor. "Reading a novel?"

"Maybe writing one," chimed in someone from the next line over.

"*War and Pees*!" suggested one runner, shifting her weight from foot to foot.

"*Jacob's Bladder*!" shouted another.

"*Brave Poo World*," said Starling, before adding, "OK, this isn't funny anymore."

Just as she and a few others were preparing to call 9-1-1

because, as Starling said, "I swear she must have died in there," the door swung open and its occupant stepped out, rubbing antibacterial gel on her hands.

"Finally," Starling muttered, before entering the porta potty herself.

Witnesses reported she remained inside for seven and a half minutes before emerging.

Man Sets World Record for Running Marathon While Mansplaining

October 24, 2017

For Lee Majors, finishing last Sunday's Sommerstown Marathon was doubly triumphant. When he crossed the line in a time of 3:38:27, the Austin resident notched a personal record—and also became the fastest runner ever to complete a marathon while mansplaining nonstop.

The previous record for fastest marathon while mansplaining was 3:55:14, set at the 2015 Steamtown Marathon in Scranton, Pennsylvania.

For Majors, it was a natural goal to pursue. The 33-

year-old, a self-described "tech bro" who works at an internet start-up, told reporters after the race that he's been patiently explaining things to women for as long as he can remember.

"That's where *mansplain* comes from, actually," he told a woman standing nearby. "From the words *man* and *explain*."

A veteran of five previous marathons with a PR, before Sunday, of 3:45, Majors also knew he had the physical ability to beat the previous record.

Still, it wasn't an easy feat.

First, said Majors, he had trouble finding training partners.

"I think I went through six or seven woman friends in my first two months of training," he said. "They were all strong runners, but each of them quit after, like, one long run with me. Which was weird."

He paused to wave over a petite East African woman who had just stepped down from the winners' podium.

"Long runs are important when you're training for a marathon," he told her, slowly.

"It helps you build endurance," he added, as handlers bundled her away.

The race itself also presented challenges. Two independent observers had to accompany Majors by bicycle "every step of the way" to monitor Majors' output, said Oscar Goldman, a spokesperson for Guinness World Records.

"Any lapse in mansplaining [during the race] would have resulted in a disqualification," Goldman said. "It had to be a constant stream of condescending explanation, preferably on a topic already well understood by the listener."

Majors accomplished that and then some, beginning in the starting corral, where he told the woman next to him that "the marathon is actually 26.2 miles, not just 26" and continuing well into the finishers chute, where he described to a female volunteer, a graduate student in engineering, how space blankets work.

In between, Majors kept the pace—of running and mansplaining—steady. During a surprise bathroom stop around mile 16, observers listened while Majors, from inside a portable toilet, shouted to a group of women watching the race, "Actually, when the little dial on the door is red, that means the toilet is occupied."

En route to his dual records Majors also mansplained scores of other things, including tailwinds, electronic timing mats, electrolytes, and the story of Pheidippides.

"There was no shortage of ladies on the course," he said, "and no shortage of things to explain to them."

Asked what's next, Majors laughed and said he was most interested in a beer and a cheeseburger.

After that?

"I'd like to work on my speed, maybe get that PR down to a sub-3:35," he said.

"By the way," he said, looking directly at a female journalist, "PR stands for 'personal record.' And *sub* means 'under.'"

"Course Was Long," Complains Marathoner Whose Own Serpentine Path Along Route Looks Like Something Out of "Family Circus"

October 29, 2017

Loudly voicing her displeasure as she crossed the finish line, a competitor at Sunday's Mansfield Park Marathon declared the course "long."

"Come on!" said Elizabeth Bennet, 26, slowing to a walk and checking her smartwatch. "Twenty-six point *seven?*"

For Bennet, who finished in 4 hours 22 minutes 35 seconds, it was an unpleasant end to a race she'd spent dodging fellow runners; darting across the road to grab water, hug friends, and take selfies; swinging wide around the course's many turns; and, at one point, doubling back to retrieve a hat she'd dropped.

A standard marathon is 26.219 miles long (42.195 kilometers). Race directors sometimes add a few feet per mile, applying the short course prevention factor "to ensure that the measured length of a course is at least as long as the desired length."

Sunday's course was, in fact, almost exactly 26.219

miles in length, run along its tangents, as certified by USA Track & Field.

"LONG!!!" Bennet wrote in a Facebook post in which she shared GPS data of her run, including a map that traced her path along the course. The map depicts a frenetic scribble in the first half-mile, apparently as Bennet weaved her way through a crowded field, followed over the remaining miles by a series of lazy arcs, meandering curves, and detours that call to mind the circuitous "dotted line" rambles undertaken by the distractible children in the classic comic strip "Family Circus."

"I will never run this garbage race again. They can't even get the distance right!"

Bennet's route appears to show her deviating from the course to, among other things, take advantage of a swing set, greet a friendly dog, and check out a tree house.

After publishing her Facebook comments, Bennet returned her attention to those around her in the finish line area.

"I can't believe you ran us *half a mile* too long!" Bennet told a volunteer outside the medical tent. "I hope someone gets fired over this."

This Mother of Six Just Ran Her 10th Sub-3:00 Marathon, You Lazy Piece of Shit

November 6, 2017

Veronica Corningstone is a busy woman.

The 42-year-old mother of six, a marketing manager in San Diego, starts her days well before sunrise, waking early to log at least 5 miles while her husband, Ron, and the kids sleep. Then she showers, dresses, rouses her children, packs lunches, feeds the family's two dogs, gets the kids off to school, and is at work by 8 a.m. Evenings are similarly packed. Weekend long runs begin as early as 4:30 a.m. to allow time for shuttling kids to and from playdates and various other commitments.

And on Sunday, she ran her 10th consecutive sub-3-hour marathon, you lazy piece of shit.

"It's all about prioritizing and time management," said Corningstone in an interview shortly after finishing the Ankerman Marathon in 2 hours 55 minutes 54 seconds, while you were probably sitting around in your bathrobe, eating doughnut holes. "It's about wanting something bad enough to make it happen."

Corningstone said it helps that her husband does "at least 50%" of the child-rearing, shopping, housework, and meal preparation, as compared to your own garbage spouse, who likely can't be bothered to clear his own dishes, much less rinse them off and load them into the dishwasher.

"But at the end of the day, I'm the one logging the miles," she said, which is more than can be said for the rest of you goldbricking layabouts, who want everything handed to you.

Her children, ranging in age from 12 years to 18 months, are her biggest cheerleaders, Corningstone added.

"They know that this is important to me," she said, "and that I'm a better Mommy when I run." Better than those other mommies, who wallow in indolence the way hogs wallow in filth.

What's next for Corningstone, now that she's notched her 10th sub-3:00 marathon?

"A nice recovery period, and then training for number 11!" she said, you pathetic sluggard.

Ask Dr. Dumb: How Can I Avoid Running Injuries?

February 11, 2016

Readers, today we are thrilled to introduce a new column called Ask Dr. Dumb.

Dr. Dumb will appear on this website from time to time to field questions on various topics, from training and injury prevention to nutrition and excessive flatulence. In addition, he will weigh in on the latest health and fitness research, helping you understand the findings and apply them to your daily lives.

He may also occasionally ask you for money—"just a few bucks" till he "gets back on his feet." We recommend that you ignore such requests. Trust us on this one.

Although Dr. Dumb is not an actual doctor, he often Googles things written by actual doctors. Also, he is quite tall and has a firm handshake. So we figure he knows what he's doing.

For this inaugural Dr. Dumb Q&A, the topic is Injuries and How to Prevent Them, inspired by a recent column in *The New York Times*. Let's dive right in.

Dumb Runner: Just curious—are you any relation to a Dr. Daily?
Dr. Dumb: Never heard of him.

How do you define "running injury"?

There is no single, universally accepted definition. Most often when someone refers to running injuries they mean problems caused by overuse—runner's knee, plantar fasciitis, iliotibial band syndrome (ITBS), and so on. Me, I take a more expansive view. If you hurt yourself while running, that is a running injury.

So if I trip and fall, scraping my elbow?

Running injury.

Run smack into a parked UPS truck?

Running injury.

Get sucker-punched by the guy whose wife I've been fooling around with?

Sucker-punched while you're running?

Yes.

Running injury.

According to that *New York Times* column, "as many as 90% of runners miss training time every year due to injury." Is that accurate?

It's impossible to say with any certainty. But no.

You think that number, 90%, is too high?

Too low! Just from my own experience, I know that when I ask around for someone to join me for a run, at least 90% of the time I hear, "Sorry, can't, injured." It's remarkable how often I hear that. Then again, many of these injuries must be very short-lived, because I often see these very people out running, alone or with others, shortly thereafter. Sometimes the same day.

Other sources have their own numbers—"nearly 80% of runners are injured each year," or "up to half," or 19.4% or 66%, or 37% to 56%.[1] How do you explain these discrepancies?
I explain them by asserting that no one has any idea what he's doing, that the world is run by impostors who skate by on dumb luck and delusions, and that most of what you read is nonsense.

That is a bleak assessment.
It's best not to think about it.

The *New York Times* column describes a new study that examined veteran runners who have never been injured. It found that these runners landed much more "lightly" when they ran, resulting in less impact—even if they were heel-strikers.
Is there a question in there somewhere?

What do you make of these findings?
Not surprising, I guess. Seems intuitive that pounding hard with each stride, as if you're trying to stomp to death an endless series of scorpions, is not a smart way to run.

The column also refers to "running-injury virgins."
I hope their first time is special.

---

[1] The stats really do vary that widely.

To run more lightly, the column suggests that you imagine you're running on eggshells. Does it matter if they're white eggs or brown?
No. The idea that brown eggshells are any healthier to run on than white eggshells is a myth.

Does stretching help to prevent injuries?
No.

Foam rolling?
No.

Massage?
No.

Ice baths?
Yes!

Really?
No. Listen, you can do that stuff if you want to. You can also purchase a magic wand and wave it over your legs before every run if it makes you feel better. Same effect.

Then what is the best way to prevent running injuries?
Don't overthink it. Run relaxed, the way your body wants to. Increase your mileage very slowly. Take days off. If something hurts, stop. Rest until it doesn't hurt anymore. Even if that means not running for a few days. And for God's sake, don't fool around with other people's spouses.

Any parting words?
Yes. If your readers are interested in purchasing a magic wand, have them contact me via DumbRunner.com. I have several models available, including High Density, Textured, Gluten Free, and Travel Size.[1]

Thank you, Dr. Dumb.
You're welcome. Be well.

---

[1] Just kidding! Or am I...? (I am.)

The Dumb Runner Guide to Turning Your Kids Into Awesome Runners

April 20, 2016

Everyone knows that kids naturally love to run. Unfortunately, as everyone also knows, kids are lazy crybabies who will whine and moan at the first sign of discomfort, insisting on taking a "break."

Given these confounding facts, how can we most effectively push our kids to be their absolute best? Is a small child even capable of understanding that breaks are for losers, which is what they'll be if they stop their workout barely halfway through—a loser? Will purchasing a professional-grade 50-watt handheld bullhorn with siren[1] help them understand this?

The answer to all of the above is a resounding yes. Well, that's the answer to the last two, anyway.

As always, Dumb Runner is here to help. Follow these guidelines and your child will be an awesome runner before you know it.

First, Dispense With This Idea of "Fun"
The number one mistake that parents of young runners make is to stress that running should be fun, that just "getting out there and trying" is the important thing. And then they wonder why their kids suck at running.

Mom and Dad, the impulse to shield your child from pain and disappointment is understandable. But it is misguided. Because there is no greater pain and disappointment than realizing, as a teen or young adult, that you are an awful runner because your parents didn't love you enough to scream at you to get back out there and give them another 2 miles because placing fourth—fourth!—in the Firecracker Festival 1-mile kids' run is an embarrassment to them, to you, and to your community.

Running is many things. "Fun" is not one of them! Reinforce this message daily, via your bullhorn.

Use Games to Build Strength, Speed, and Endurance
One of our favorites is a little game we call "If You Can Run All the Way Around the Track Before Daddy's Watch Beeps, Daddy Won't Throw Away Your Doll."

---

[1] They're surprisingly affordable.

Skip the Jogging Stroller

Some experts may tell you to "start your kids early," at age 1 or 2, by introducing them to running via jogging strollers. This is absurd. Kids that young are much too short to push a jogging stroller with any success. Focus instead on agility drills and running laps around your house.

Don't Use Running as a Punishment

In many sports, coaches treat running like a punishment, ordering an athlete to "go run 10 laps" for goofing off or getting something wrong. This is counterproductive, as it trains the youngster to associate running with dread or disapproval.

Instead, treat running as a reward. Motivate your child by saying, for instance, "Jackson, I swear, if you fall off pace one more time I'm gonna give you a reward you'll never forget!"

Remember That Young Brains Are Still Developing

This means you may need to use simple words, and shout, to make yourself understood when communicating with your child.

e.g.,

"Faster!"

"No, *faster*!"

"You want a birthday party next month? Then go faster!"[1]

---

[1] *Star Wars* fans: Think Grand Moff Tarkin telling Leia, aboard the Death Star, "You would prefer another target, a military target? Then *name the system!*"

Use Appropriate Terminology

Experts agree that parents should avoid using euphemisms when referring to genitals. So telling little Johnny before his 20x400 repeats that you expect him to go "balls to the wall" is frowned upon. Instead, command him to go "testicles to the wall."

Learn This One Invaluable Line

"Oh, what are you gonna do? Cry?"

This may be the single most useful retort that parents of young runners have at their disposal. It works well in any number of difficult situations, including those in which your child is already crying.

For added effect, pretend in an exaggerated manner that you are crying as well.

Later, in a quiet moment, take your child aside. Explain gently that tears are really "weakness juice" and that only stupid crybabies make weakness juice come out of their eyes when things get tough.

Then have your child drop and give you 20.

Be Generous With Praise

Children respond to praise, and yours crave your approval more than you probably know. So when you notice a child running well, be sure to point this out to your own kid.

"Wow, look at him go," you might tell your child. "He is really running fast. His parents must be so proud of him."

Know That Other Parents May Have Different Ideas About Kids and Running

Some parents or so-called "experts" may express concern

or even alarm at how hard you're pushing your child to run. These people are trying to psych you out. They know how awesome your child is going to be at running and they are jealous. Tune them out.

Then have your child drop and give you 20.

Ask Dr. Dumb: How Can I Mix Sex and Jogging?

December 7, 2016

Readers!

We're sorry to shout. But today is a very exciting day. Because today we reintroduce Ask Dr. Dumb, a column that we launched with some fanfare back in February.

After that initial column, titled "How Can I Avoid Running Injuries?," we revisited Dr. Dumb three times in March and April. ("Did Nike Bribe Kenyan Officials?"; "Are Juice Cleanses Really Worthless?"; "Should Runners Eat Peeps?") (Answers: Maybe; No; Not if you're smart.)

Then we just stopped publishing Ask Dr. Dumb. Weird, right?

Anyway, that's all behind us. Today we welcome Dr. Dumb back with open arms, no questions asked. And not a moment too soon, because today's topic is: "Jogging" and sex.

This is a biggie, so let's start nice and slow.

Dumb Runner: Dr. Dumb, welcome back.
Dr. Dumb: Thank you.

Today's topic is "jogging" and sex, and—
Wait. Why did you just make air quotes around *jogging*?

We will tell you why. Because today's topic is inspired by a recent Craigslist Personals ad that we stumbled across.
"Stumbled across." Right.

The subject line of this ad was, and we quote: "I need a 'jogging' partner (Demver)"
Demver?

Yes.
Where the hell is Demver?

We believe it's somewhere near Colorado Sprimgs.
Huh.

Anyway, you soon learn why the word *jogging* is in quotation marks when you read the ad itself.
Do you have a screen grab of the ad, in case it gets deleted?

Yes. And here it is:

> **I need a "jogging" partner (Demver)**
>
> I have two issues in my life that I'm looking to fix with this post. First, and we're starting with the easier thing to fix here, is that I need to exercise more. So I've decided that I need to start going for a run every morning, nothing intense at first, but gradually building up to something longer. And to motivate me I need someone to do this with. Maybe a woman, who's roughly my age, and is also looking for motivation to workout.
>
> age: 34
>
> Second, and this is where you'll probably judge me as being an awful human being, I have a non-existent sex life. And I'm married, and pretty happily. Which makes fixing that problem... hard. I'm sure there are also women out there who are roughly my age and in very similar situations.
>
> My brilliant solution to this is that you and I fix both these problems at the same time. Get up really early in the morning, say 5:00 or so, and head out for a jog. And then run into each other at one of the nice wooded areas near here (Wash park? Downtown?) which are great for jogging. And then halfway through the we take a little break and get to know each other a bit. This, like the jog itself, can start simple and escalate over time. Just stand around and chat for a bit at first. But as we know, the talking leads to touching. And the touching leads to sex. And then... uh, more jogging I suppose?
>
> I'm in decent, but not great, shape right now (hence the need to start jogging). About 6 foot and 175 pounds, glasses sometimes.... And I'm looking for a woman who's similar to me - roughly my age, in decent shape but looking to exercise more, and looking for a bit more excitement out of life. If this sounds like an interesting idea we should talk some more.
>
> • do NOT contact me with unsolicited services or offers

Jeepers!

Our thoughts exactly. So our first question to you, Dr. Dumb, is this: Just how common is this sort of thing?
Screen grabs? Very common. Easy, too. On a Mac you just hit SHIFT-COMMAND-4, and—

No. We mean "jogging."
Jogging? Or "jogging"?

"Jogging."
It's quite rare, if my own experience is any indication. I can count on one hand the number of times I've stopped during a run to have sex in a wooded area with a semi-anonymous partner.

How does something like this come to happen?
Well, the guy in the ad nails it, as guys on Craigslist usually do. You post something online then sit back and wait for replies to roll in. It helps if you mention that you're married and in "not great" shape. Also, if you suggest meeting this stranger at 5 a.m. in a wooded area. After that, you just sit back and wait for the responses to roll in.

Would this be a good place to make a Body Glide joke?
Good a place as any.

In your experience, does "talking lead to touching, and touching lead to sex"?
Oh, yes. This is why I'm very careful who I talk to.

Well, Dr. Dumb, thank you for your "time."
You're "welcome."

Man's Anecdote Contradicts Research on Knee Health

January 23, 2017

Conventional wisdom has long held that running is "bad for your knees." A recent study, widely publicized last week, made headlines by suggesting just the opposite—that running might actually be beneficial for the joint.

Now, however, the scientists behind that study are publicly questioning their work and have asked the journal that published the findings to scrub their report from its website.

"New information has come to light which contradicts our own conclusions on running and knee health," said Dr. Gordon Sumner, lead researcher of the study. "This information is compelling and too powerful to ignore."

The information in question came in the form of a reader comment[1] on a news article reporting on the study:

"We saw that," Dr. Sumner said, "and it stopped us

---

[1] Yes, that is the actual comment.

cold. Now we don't know what to think.

"It just goes to show you," he continued, "that you can design and carry out a study as carefully as you like, have it published in a peer-reviewed journal, presenting your data and providing context and analysis...you can take all of those steps, and then along comes a personal anecdote from some guy and everything collapses.

"Guess it's back to the drawing board for us."

News of the devastating anecdote spread like wildfire throughout the scientific community.

"It's every medical researcher's worst nightmare," said Dr. Stewart Copeland, spokesperson for the International Association of Research Scientists. "All of that careful work, undone in a few keystrokes by Ron from Texas.

"But," he said, "that's science for you."

Ask Dr. Dumb: Are Juice Cleanses Really Worthless?

April 26, 2016

Readers, lately you may have noticed headlines like "That Super Expensive Juice Cleanse Does Nothing," or "Juicing Is Officially Over," or "Prince Died Without a Will, According to Court Documents."[1]

And because of this, you must be thinking, *What? How does someone that rich and famous not have a simple will drawn up?* And, *Now who will decide who gets all his stuff?* And, *He must have, like, dozens of guitars, just for starters.*

Well, let's put that aside for now. The topic of today's column is juicing. Not Prince. We're sorry we even mentioned Prince.[2] Let's move on.

Anyway—juicing. It's been getting a bad rap recently, thanks to articles like the ones cited above, and another titled "Fancy Juice Doesn't Cleanse the Body of Toxins," from the *New York Times*, which begins:

To say that drinking juice detoxifies the body isn't quite the same as claiming leeches suck out poisons, but it's fairly close.

That article goes on to say that juicing, which has become very fashionable and very lucrative, is pretty much

---

[1] All real headlines!

[2] We are not sorry we mentioned Prince.

a load of bunk.

Is it really, though? To find out, we turned to our in-house expert on all things juicy, Dr. Dumb.

Dumb Runner: What do you make of stories suggesting that "fancy juice" does not actually rid the body of toxins?
Dr. Dumb: Those stories are seriously flawed.

How so?
They completely fail to take into account the degree of fanciness of the juices in question.

So the quality of the juice makes a difference?
Absolutely. If the juice you're drinking isn't ridding your body of toxins, I think you have to ask yourself, "Is my juice fancy enough?" I mean, there's fancy juice and there's fancy juice. If you know what I mean.

I don't. What makes one juice fancier than another?
A number of variables are used in determining a juice's Fanciness Quotient. The place of purchase, for instance—juices bought at, say, Whole Foods are inherently more fancy than those bought at Safeway or your local convenience store or other lesser purveyors of foodstuffs whose aisles are vaguely dingy and whose lighting is unflattering and probably fluorescent. Same goes for any ingredients bought to make your own juice at home.

Another variable is price. The more you pay, the fancier the juice. Which I suppose goes without saying.

Beyond that—and this is very interesting—certain aesthetic factors come into play. Any given juice becomes

20 to 40% fancier if it's blended or consumed by, or near, an attractive woman in a bright, tastefully appointed kitchen at a blonde-wood island displaying an array of fresh fruits and vegetables.

There's another factor, but it's harder to pin down. Some juices just have a certain je ne sais pas about them.

Don't you mean, "a certain je ne sais quoi"?
I don't know.

So juice that's truly fancy is the key to an effective juice cleanse.
Yes, but you also need a fancy blender. Plus a fancy glass to pour your juice into before you smile at it and then consume it.

Let's step back for a moment. When we say that a certain juice cleanses the body of toxins, how are we defining *toxin*?
A toxin is defined as "something very bad that is in your body doing its bad little things." Here is a sketch of a toxin that I did for a lecture I gave in Paris earlier this year:

Actual toxins are much smaller, of course. Maybe half that size.

By the way, this is the same standard definition that some massage therapists use when they say that massage "releases toxins" from our muscles and that drinking a Dixie cup of water afterward will help to "flush the toxins" from our blood.

Are these massage therapists crazy?
Yes. But don't tell them so, especially when you're facedown on their table and they have their knee in your back.

How, exactly, does very fancy juice cleanse the body of toxins?
The toxins are simply overwhelmed with fanciness. Our toxins just are not equipped to handle it. Un-fancy juice? Sure. Somewhat-fancy? Usually. Very fancy? No. From an evolutionary standpoint, basically, toxins have not kept up with developments in fancy juicing.

Does this suggest that our toxins are capable of playing catch-up, of mutating to the point where even really fancy juices can't overcome them?
That is a concern, yes. This is why scientists are racing to develop "superfancy juices" that will literally drown the body's toxins in a tidal wave of blended fruit-and-vegetable fanciness.

Did the Tour de France recently land an official "juice partner"?
Yes, it did.

I thought they were trying to put that sort of thing

behind them.
You're thinking of another kind of juice.

Thank you for your time, Dr. Dumb. As always, this has been an illuminating conversation.
You're very welcome.

Marathon Champ's Secret: A Surprisingly Simple Diet

May 24, 2016

Everyone knows that Africans dominate long-distance running. It's apparent simply by looking at the results of just about any major marathon over the past couple of decades.

(A closer look at the numbers illustrates just how dominant. According to the Science of Sport, "the percentage of top 100 performances in the world each year belonging to Africans went from 16% in 1990 to 94% in 2011.")

What you might not know is what fuels these performances—and how ridiculously simple it is.

"I grew up very poor," says Simon Kiptanui, 25, a top Kenyan marathoner. "Like most families, our diet was a little bit of meat, lots of vegetables, sometimes eggs from our chickens, but always ugali."

Ugali, a traditional Kenyan dish, is a "stiff porridge" made of cornmeal and water. It is a staple of Kenyan meals, sometimes called that country's national dish.

Kiptanui's diet is not unusual. Most Kenyan distance runners grow up eating cheap, basic, filling food like ugali.

"This has been my diet all my life," says Kiptanui, shrugging. "It is really all you need to perform well as a runner.

"Oh!" he continues, reacting to what seems like a kick under the table from his agent. "I mean, that and Opti-GLYCO® Trip-X Surge Tabs™ from PhX Labs, now available in new Mango Explosion flavor. Are you ready to #FeeltheSurge?

"Yes," he says, nodding his head. "Opti-GLYCO® Trip-X Surge Tabs™ are crucial for success for sure."

Kiptanui feels that many runners in the West overthink things like diet and nutrition.

"Simple, basic things like ugali, vegetable stews, bread, and tea have fueled East African runners for many years, and with great success," he says. "I never saw a need to add complex dishes to my diet, or to add dubious supplements.

"Except," he hastens to add, rubbing his knee, "for Opti-GLYCO® Trip-X Surge Tabs™, which help me recover and keep me Fueled for Life™. When I mix my Opti-GLYCO® Trip-X Surge Tabs™ in 8 ounces of water, all I have to do is sit back, enjoy the natural flavors, and prepare to #FeeltheSurge."

On a typical day, Kiptanui says, he will wake and have tea with milk and sugar along with some bread or ugali left over from the previous night. Lunch and dinner likely will involve ugali along with a bit of lean meat or eggs for protein.

"And a glass of water with my Opti-GLYCO® Trip-X Surge Tabs™," he says. "Of course.

"The night before a race," he says, "I may have rice or pasta instead of ugali. For a special treat, instead of my usual Ice Lime Opti-GLYCO® Trip-X Surge Tabs™ made with natural flavors, I will have some Strawberry-Kiwi Lemonade Opti-GLYCO® Trip-X Surge Tabs™ made with natural flavors."

During a marathon itself, Kiptanui explains, he doesn't drink much of anything.

"Until I am ready to #FeeltheSurge, that is," he says. "Then I go for a bottle prepared with Opti-GLYCO® Trip-X Surge Tabs™, soon to be available in convenient chewable form, with flavors including Banana Berry, Piña Colada, and Razz-Ma-Blast."

He sighs.

"For more, visit Opti-GLYCO® on the web," he says, "or follow them on Facebook and Twitter."

These Muffins Will Make You Say "Holy Shit, These Are Good Muffins"

July 25, 2016

If you're anything like us, you love a good muffin—but don't love the fat and sugar they're usually loaded with.

Well, have we got a muffin for you.

These muffins have cranberries, we guess, and instead of the "chemicals" found in store-bought baked goods these contain stuff that's good for you. Flaxseed or something. Probably some superfoods in there, too.

But, holy shit, they are so good. You won't believe it.

Did you get a load of that photo? Admit it—the photo is why you clicked the link, right?[1] Because you saw that photo and thought to yourself, *Damn, those are some tasty-looking muffins.*

Can't you just imagine peeling back those muffin cup liners and sinking your teeth into that warm, crumb-topped goodness? Yeah, you can. Don't they look moist? Yeah, they do. Doesn't that bowl of fresh cranberries in the background, in soft focus, convey a sense of homemade wholesomeness? You bet your ass it does.

The fact that this article was shared by a running website probably also had you thinking, *You know what, those muffins must also be sort of healthy. Tasty muffins without the guilt? Uh, hello? Win-win!*

Then you thought, *I will click that link then skim the article and print it out or email it to myself so I can remember later to make these muffins. Maybe this weekend.*

Well, that is completely understandable. Because wow, these muffins.

Plus, they make a great breakfast "on the go." Just toss a couple of these in your bag or backpack and you are all set. Morning, fueled.

You could even throw them at friends and family members, from a distance. They might be annoyed at first—like, "What the hell, why'd you just throw that at me?"—until, that is, they retrieve the muffin and take a bite. Then they would understand why you threw that at them.

A couple of warnings:
- If you are allergic to deliciousness, you'd better

---

[1] You'll have to imagine you clicked a link to read this. Work with us here.

steer clear of these muffins, because they are absolutely packed with it.

- You should probably not eat these muffins in public or at work, unless you have an office with a door and the door is closed. Because every time you take a bite you will scream, "Holy shit, these are good muffins!" or "Are you f***ing kidding me with this taste?"

In rare cases, people consuming these muffins have reported spontaneous orgasm.

Anyway, we wish we could find the recipe. It was around here somewhere.

Man Takes Break to Fuel Up While Shopping for Fuel

January 10, 2017

A local man recently paused for nourishment while shopping for sports nutrition products at a Safeway supermarket.

"You gotta stay fueled up," said Marcus Brody, 32, a personal trainer and veteran of numerous Warrior Dash 5K obstacle runs. "Just like a race car, you know? Fuel."

Brody was at the Safeway, he said, to pick up a few items including energy gels, sport beans, coconut water, whey-protein bars, recovery drink powder, and a case of sports drink, when his Fitbit beeped.

"It goes off every 15 minutes to remind me when to fuel up," he said. "It's important to space out your intake of carbs just right."

Brody popped several "ancient grain" pretzels into his mouth and took a long drink from a bottle of blue liquid.

"Fueling is so important," he said, wiping his mouth with the back of his hand. "Electrolytes, too. Need to replenish your body's store of electrolytes. It's all part of a smart fueling strategy."

Then, noting with alarm that he had worked out some 20 minutes earlier but hadn't yet ingested any protein, he grabbed a whey-protein bar from his basket, opened its package, and tore off a large bite.

"Normally I wouldn't eat food I haven't paid for yet," he said, "but you've got to get some protein within 30 minutes of working out. For recovery."

Experts agree with Brody's approach to fueling.

"Fueling is key to optimal performance," said Marion Ravenwood, a registered nutri-specialist, Certified Sports Fueling Coach, spokesperson for the American Council of Electrolyte Experts, and adviser to the PowerBar-Gatorade Institute for the Study of Performance Optimization.

"Fuel," she added.

Back in the aisles of the Safeway, Brody was crossing the final items off his list—with one exception.

"I was hoping to grab a box of Opti-GLYCO® Trip-X Surge Tabs™," he said, "but I guess Safeway doesn't carry them."

Brody's next stop, then, was a Vitamin Shoppe store across town.

"First, though, I'm gonna crush this Vanilla Crisp energy bar," he said. "Gotta fuel up."

Man Carb-Loading for 5K Has No Idea Why He's Not Losing Weight

February 13, 2017

Like many people who take up running, Dirk Benedict expected to drop a few pounds thanks to his newfound pursuit.

"That was a big reason I chose running in the first place," said Benedict, a 34-year-old graphic designer who pledged to be more active this year and to get rid of the "spare tire" he'd acquired thanks to long hours at work, lots of junk food, and virtually no exercise.

That has not happened. In fact, Benedict said, he has actually gained a few pounds.

"I don't get it," he said during a recent interview at the Pasta Barn, a restaurant in his hometown of Doylestown, Pennsylvania. "I've been running for almost six weeks now, training for this race. I even do some of that High Intensity Interval Training, which is supposed to incinerate calories. And I'm heavier than ever."

The race in question is the Doylestown Dash, a 5K.

"I'm on this training plan," he said. "I've been following it religiously, doing, like, 20 miles a week. I've been stretching, resting, hydrating. It's a total lifestyle change, you know?

"And," he added, gesturing to the plate of fettuccine in

front of him, "I'm carb-loading, obviously. You've gotta fuel up for race day."

The 5K will be Benedict's first race of any distance and, he says, he's determined not to hit the dreaded "wall." In addition to loading up on carbs, he has developed a fueling plan for the race.

"I did some research and discovered the race only has two aid stations," he said. "So I'll have my FuelBelt and some gels."

Benedict paused, grumbling as he loosened his belt.

"Man," he said, "I'll be glad when the weight loss kicks in."

He then asked a server for more breadsticks.

Holy Shit, Look at These New Running Shoes!

March 14, 2016

Holy shit,[1] guys! It's a new running shoe!

Have you *seen* this new running shoe? It's new! Also, it's slightly different somehow from the previous model! And it looks sort of wild! You're practically guaranteed to do a spit take when you see it! Or a double take! Or ma,ybe both! Like a double-spit-take! Where you're drinking a beverage when you happen to notice this new running shoe out of the corner of your eye, and you're like, "Whoa!"[2] and you spew your beverage all over the place, then you immediately take another sip but you accidentally notice the new shoe once more and, uh oh, here we go again!

I don't know about you, but I can't wait to get my hands on a pair of these new running shoes! God, I want them so bad!

Until that can happen, though, I need to find some sort of video on the internet about this new shoe! One where I can see this new shoe being held by someone who's talking

---

[1] I didn't realize how often I use the word *shit* until I put this book together. Sorry.

[2] There is no such word as *woah*. *Woah* looks dumb. Stop using *woah*.

about this new shoe! Maybe he will hold the new shoe up to the camera as he talks about the new shoe and bend it to show me how flexible it is!

Man, this new shoe makes my current shoes look like garbage! What was I thinking when I bought those garbage shoes? Guess I wasn't! I will throw open my window and hurl my current shoes out at the first opportunity!

Better yet: I will hike to the top of an active volcano and throw my shoes into it! Good-bye and good riddance, stupid old shoes! That's what you get for not being a game changer!

I have so many questions about this new running shoe! Like, what kind of ride does it deliver? A smooth one? What's the drop? Like, how many millimeters? Four? Eight? *How many?* And what sort of foam, exactly, is that midsole made of? Does it have properties of some kind that I should know about? Are these properties new, too?

Somebody, please, write something about this new running shoe ASAP! Better yet, a bunch of somebodies please write a bunch of somethings! Because I will read it all! When it comes to this new running shoe, my appetite cannot and will not be sated!

How much does this new running shoe cost? Who cares! Whatever it is, it's a bargain at twice the price! It's a new running shoe!

In conclusion, let me sum up:

New running shoe!

How to Buy Running Shoes

September 7, 2016

Few things are as bewildering as setting out to buy a pair of running shoes. Even a small running store will have dozens of brands and models. Which pair is right for you? The blue ones? The red ones? The ones with stripes? Argh!

The whole process can be overwhelming. But it doesn't have to be. Armed with the right knowledge, you can quickly narrow your choices down to a relative handful and, ultimately, walk out of the store with a pair of running shoes that you will love and that will love you back.

This guide will guide you. Consider it your guide.

The Basics

- Running shoes are divided into eight basic categories: Cushioned, neutral, stability, acoustic, extra-strength, crunchy, smooth, and big & tall. Each kind of shoe is designed for a very particular kind of runner.
- To determine your foot type, try the "wet test"—put a large piece of paper on the ground, wet the soles of your bare feet, then carefully step onto the paper and back off of it. Roll the paper tightly, light one end, and smoke it. Soon a wraithlike Steve Prefontaine will materialize and whisper your foot type into your ear. His moustache may tickle, so be prepared.

- Buy the most expensive shoes you can afford. As one expert points out, "Things that cost a lot of money are better than things that don't cost a lot of money."
- Do not try on shoes at a specialty running store and then walk out and order them online to save a few bucks. People who do that are dicks.

Preparing for Your Visit

- Be sure to take your current running shoes with you. The salesperson can learn a lot about you and your running style just by smelling them.
- Also bring along a list of any prescription or over-the-counter medications you're taking.
- Wear the socks you usually run in. Resist the temptation to impress a salesperson by showing off your fanciest hosiery!
- Likewise, take several pairs of pants with you to the store—blue jeans, khakis, cords, etc. You'll want to choose a running shoe versatile enough to look good with all of them.
- Phone ahead and ask the store whether their credit card reader's chip thing is operable, or if you just swipe, or what. This will save time and potential embarrassment later.

At the Store

- Signal your intentions by standing awkwardly, in silence, near the shoes until someone notices you.
- Test the salesperson's knowledge. Ask, "Is this the

right shoe or the left one?" A pro will be able to answer immediately.

- Have a salesperson watch you run. She may notice little things about your form that you won't, or can't. For instance, she might see that instead of running forward you sidle like a crab. (If so, you'll want shoes with plenty of lateral stability.)
- Skip the undercoating. It's a scam.
- Take your time. Choosing the right running shoes is a big deal, so don't let a salesperson pressure you into a decision just because you've been there for two and a half hours and the store is "closing."
- Drive a hard bargain. Running store salespeople love it when customers haggle. If you can't get a cash discount, try asking them to throw in something free with your purchase, like a pair of socks or a taco.

Enjoy your new shoes!

New Product for Runners Serves No Apparent Purpose

November 28, 2016

With the holiday shopping season now in full swing, running enthusiasts are sharing their wish lists and picking up gifts for fellow runners. This year, however, amid the usual assortment of apparel, gear, gadgets, and accessories, they're eyeing something new—the RunStrap.

Available in three sizes and half a dozen colors, RunStrap is "sturdy, TSA-friendly, and hand-stitched right here in the USA," according to its manufacturer, Metku LLC.

And it's quickly becoming the season's hottest gift, say retailers and industry analysts, despite the fact that it serves no obvious function.

"I can't remember the last time runners went this crazy for a new piece of gear," says Richard Vernon, CEO of the National Association of Retailers Who Sell Sports Stuff. "Especially one that, by all outward appearances, doesn't actually do anything."

This lack of utility hasn't deterred holiday shoppers.

"Yeah, I'm not sure what it's for," said Claire Standish, 24, a runner who was shopping Friday at B.C. Running, a Shermer, Illinois, running store. "But all these blogs are raving about it. And my friend Allison is a RunStrap ambassador. So, you know."

"I guess it's for stretching?" said Andrew Clark, 33 another shopper, turning a RunStrap over in his hands. "Or maybe you wear it while you run. Like a safety thing.

"Anyway," he said, "I heard they're good for recovery."

Or, perhaps, for injury prevention.

"I've been using the RunStrap for three weeks," said John Bender, a salesperson at B.C. Running. "And I haven't been injured that whole time."

The people behind RunStrap haven't done much to help clarify their product's purpose.

"Runners, Show Us How You #Strap!" the brand says in a Twitter campaign urging fans to share photos of themselves using the RunStrap. The resulting images depict runners looping the product around their feet, knotting it around their waist, removing it from their freezers, and simply holding it while they run.

Meanwhile, sales show no signs of slowing, thanks in part to RunStrap's inclusion in a "Gear of the Year" feature in *Outdoor Monthly* magazine, opposite a full-page ad for RunStrap.

Editor's Note: This post is sponsored by RunStrap.
Go to Twitter and Show Us How You #Strap!

A Runner's Guide to Running Socks for Runners

February 28, 2017

You would think, dear reader, that nothing could be simpler than a sock. What is a sock, after all, but a fabric condom for your foot, a protective barrier between skin and shoe? Just grab a pair, slip 'em on, and go... Right?

Oh, reader. Sometimes you are so naïve it's adorable.

Socks are far from simple. Like, really far. Today's socks are highly complex and come in a dizzying array of styles, made from a stunning variety of materials, designed for a vomitous number of activities.

Here is everything you need to know.

Q: As a runner, why do I need socks? Isn't the whole "wear socks" thing just propaganda from Big Sock?
A: No, runners really do need to wear socks. Otherwise, after a few miles your feet will turn to hamburger.

That sounds horrible, yet delicious.
Oh, there is nothing delicious about it. Believe me.

How many different types and brands of running socks exist?
One website lists at least 25 brands of running socks and 16 "sock types," including cold-weather socks, knee-high

socks, maximum-cushion socks, no-show socks, tab socks, and trail-running socks.[1]

That's an awful lot of socks.
You said it.

Do I really need special socks for trail running?
No.

Do I need sport-specific socks for running at all?
No.

But all these ads say—
I know what the ads say. And I'm saying, if the socks fit and are comfortable, they're fine. They don't have to be special fancy running socks.

Easy for you to say. You probably have a drawer full of special fancy running socks.
True. I do have a drawer full of special fancy running socks. It's also true that I often run in socks like these, because I'm already wearing them and I'm lazy:

---

[1] Really.

That looks ridiculous.
One of the nice things about getting older is that you stop giving a crap about things like socks, and what people think of your socks.

Because the closer you get to death, the more precious your remaining time seems, and you don't want to waste any of it worrying about trifles?
Exactly. So cram it.

Are cotton socks as bad as I've heard?
Yes. As we note in "7 Things Every New Runner MUST Have":

Don't even think of running in cotton socks. Cotton socks will make your feet bleed internally, then swell and eventually burst, sending bits of foam and shards of bone flying toward anyone unfortunate enough to be nearby. Instead choose socks made of merino wool or synthetics.

If you have cotton socks at home, burn them immediately.

Wow. Really?
No. Not really. Despite what you've heard elsewhere, cotton socks are fine for short runs. If you're going more than a few miles, though, wool or synthetics really are a smarter choice. Especially if it's raining.

I'm seeing a lot of "anatomically shaped" socks, designed specifically for the left and right foot—are those any better than traditional socks?
No. They're dumb and a needless complication and emblematic of everything that's wrong with running today.

In other words...
...these sock makers can take their anatomic shapes and cram them, yes.

How about those "toe socks," the ones with individual compartments for each of your toes?
You mean the ones that provide "a restriction-free environment," so that "your toes are able to become activated, providing you with increased dexterity, tactile sensitivity and allowing them to perform as they were intended"?[1]

Yes.
How do you think I feel about those?

And compression socks?
Dude. Please.

So I just read about these $199 Sensoria Fitness Socks, which are "infused with proprietary 100% textile sensors" and "paired with a Bluetooth Smart cool and detachable anklet that not only delivers superior accuracy in step counting, speed, calories—"[2]
If you continue talking about this product, I will punch myself in the face until I lose consciousness.

I also enjoy hunting. Do I need special socks for that?
You certainly do, and the good people at SmartWool are

---

[1] Actual quotes from actual sock website.

[2] We are not making any of this up.

here to help. Their new PhD Hunt socks feature these details (really), "each specified to (a) hunter's needs"...

- Virtually Seamless™ toe to prevent blisters and chafing
- 4 Degree Elite Fit system for a stay-put fit
- Strategically placed, gender-specific ventilation zones
- Luxurious terry loop knit for breathability and moisture management
- 21-micron fiber knit for ultimate next-to-skin comfort
- Light, medium, and heavy cushioning for a range of conditions
- Taller crews and silhouettes for each hunt activity
- Patented Indestructawool™ technology for durability

We tested the PhD Hunt socks in the Dumb Runner Lab and found that they are nearly seven times huntier than non-hunting socks:

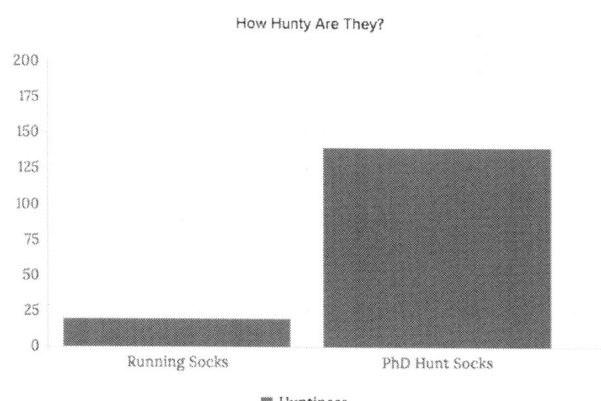

Can't argue with data like that.

What if I'm out for a run in my running socks and I spot an elk that I want to shoot?
In that scenario obviously you would have to stop and change your socks. Quick, too, before the elk gets away.

What do I do with my gun while I'm changing my socks?
For firearm-related questions, please refer to "Running With Your Gun: FAQ."[1]

But what if the elk does get away and I have to run after him? Do they make socks that are designed for hunting while running?
Not yet, dear reader. Not yet.

---

[1] See page 16.

Acme Unveils Sub-2:00-Marathon Shoe

March 12, 2017

The Acme Corporation today unveiled its own entry into the "sub-2:00-marathon shoe" market—a wheeled, rocket-powered model called the Super Genius.

It's a surprise move by Acme, a quiet company based in New Mexico and known mostly for boomerangs, iron bird seed, anvils, giant magnets, and dehydrated boulders.

"No one saw this coming," said Friz Freleng, Ph.D., a professor of running shoe technology at MIT. "Nike's sub-2:00 shoe was predictable, given its 'Breaking2' project, and nobody was surprised to see Adidas follow suit.

"But Acme?" he said. "Who even knew they made athletic footwear?"

Very few people, it seems—even many Acme employees were unaware of the Super Genius. Sources tell Dumb Runner that the handful of designers and technicians working on the project, code-named "Meep Meep," signed nondisclosure agreements and worked under extremely tight supervision.

As for the shoe itself, it represents a radical departure from traditional running shoes.

For one thing, there are the wheels. Most running shoes don't have them.

"You can go faster on wheels," explained Chuck Jones,

an Acme engineer who helped to develop the Super Genius. "Faster than without wheels."

The other notable difference is the use of rocket propulsion—each shoe includes a small liquid rocket and storage for propellants.

"Acme has a world-renowned rocket science division," said Jones. "We took advantage of that in designing the Super Genius. Because rockets make things go very fast."

Also, the shoes are strapped onto the feet rather than cinched down with laces.

Reaction to Acme's shoe has been mixed, though most experts agree that, in theory and all other things being equal, the Super Genius should produce significantly faster race times.

"I don't see how a reasonably fit athlete could wear these and not break 2 hours," Dr. Freleng said. "Unless something went haywire mechanically—say, the rockets failed to ignite at the start line despite repeated attempts, causing the athlete to remove one shoe and look directly into the rocket's nozzle, shaking the thing until it suddenly ignited, scorching him with exhaust and causing his face to be blackened and his hair blown back in a comical way.

"But what are the odds that'll happen?"

"Running Is Great Because It's So Simple," Says Guy Wearing $1,170 Worth of Gear

October 11, 2017

A self-described "running junkie" has declared that he loves the sport for many reasons, but mainly because of its simplicity.

"Running is brilliant," local runner James Polk announced after a trail run Tuesday evening, pausing to stop his $400 GPS watch. "It's great because it's so simple.

"You don't need a lot of stuff," he added, unzipping his $150 lightweight thermal vest with stowable hood. "Just a pair of shoes and a road or trail."

Polk said he got into running about two years ago, after nearly a decade as a dedicated cyclist.

"That was nuts," he recalled. "You had your bike, of course, and shoes, helmet, pumps, spare tires, extra wheelsets, trainers, power meters... It just got to be too much, you know?"

Running, he said, provided a welcome relief from the complexity and expense of cycling.

"Running is elemental," he said. "We were born to run.

"There's something primal about that," he said, stowing his $115 sunglasses in his $90 hydration pack.

He gazed at the sky, closed his eyes, and breathed deep.

"It's all about remembering what's important," he said.

Polk paused to remove a pebble stuck between his $130 trail shoes and his $14 socks.

"I ran 6 miles today," he said. "Just me and nature. How awesome is that?"

The Runner's Thanksgiving BINGO Card

November 24, 2015

DUMB RUNNER *presents*

Thanksgiving Dinner BINGO for Runners

Mark off a space whenever one of your non-running relatives says...

B I N G O

I USED TO RUN BUT NOW I CAN'T	I WISH I COULD RUN	TOO MUCH IMPACT	RUNNING WILL RUIN YOUR JOINTS	RUNNING WILL RUIN YOUR KNEES
[SO-AND-SO] USED TO RUN; NOW HIS KNEES ARE SHOT	AREN'T YOUR KNEES SHOT?	DO YOU RUN EVERY DAY?	I DID A 5K MARATHON ONCE	I ONLY RUN WHEN SOMEONE'S CHASING ME
I BET YOU CAN EAT ANYTHING YOU WANT	HAVE SOME MORE— YOU'RE TOO SKINNY		YOU'LL HAVE TO RUN A MARATHON TO BURN THIS OFF!	**I'LL** HAVE TO RUN A MARATHON TO BURN THIS OFF!
DO YOU RUN EVEN WHEN IT'S HOT?	DO YOU RUN EVEN WHEN IT'S COLD?	I HATE RUNNING; IT'S SO BORING	YOU RAN A MARATHON? DID YOU WIN?	WHAT'S THE BEST RUNNING SHOE?
I READ A GUY DIED IN A MARATHON	I READ THAT, TOO	PROBABLY RUINED HIS KNEES	I GOT ONE OF THEM FITBITS	HEY, WHERE YOU GOIN'?

SPONSORED: 5 Ways to Bust Out of a Rut

January 10, 2016

Brought to You by Pratt & Whitney Commercial Jet Engines[1]

If you run long enough, sooner or later you will find yourself in a rut. That's OK. It happens to everyone. The trick is recognizing that you're in a tough spot and knowing how to pull yourself out of it. Luckily, there are several ways you can do this.

1. Take a break. Sometimes feeling burned out or bored is simply your body's way of telling you that it needs some downtime. Try a few days off, or even a week. You're a human being—not a machine, like a Pratt & Whitney PurePower® PW1000G with engine with Geared Turbofan™ technology!

2. Mix things up. Been running the same neighborhood loop, at the same pace, over and over? Tackle some new challenges, even if it's as simple as trying some new routes.

---

[1] A small part of me wondered, as I wrote this, whether someone at Pratt & Whitney would read it and laugh and send me some aircraft-grade aluminum or something. That did not happen.

If you have to bike or drive a bit to make this happen, do it. The effect it will have on your outlook will be well worth it. Heck, if you have the means, consider traveling a little farther afield—watch for bargain fares out of your local airport. Keep an eye out for flights on the Airbus A380, powered by the GP7200, a twin spool axial flow turbofan that delivers 70,000 pounds of thrust.

3. Join a group. Running with others is a surefire way to bust up your boredom. Together we're capable of much more than when we operate alone. Just look at Pratt & Whitney and General Electric Aviation, which teamed up to develop, manufacture, sell, and support a family of advanced technology engines for new high-capacity, long-range aircraft. Your local specialty running store should be able to hook you up with groups in your area.

4. Run for a greater cause. If you've never tried it, consider running a race for a charity of your choosing. This sort of external motivation may be just the "kick in the pants" you need to get out that door and excited about running again. Not quite as powerful as the kick you'll feel with the PW4000 112-inch engine, an ultra-high-thrust model covering the 74,000- to 90,000-pound thrust class—but powerful enough!

5. Set a goal. Feeling aimless? Give yourself something to aim for. Sign up for a race, or pledge to run 100 miles in a month, then give yourself a "prize" when you accomplish it. For example, a new running jacket or a PW6000 engine, which covers the 18,000- to 24,000-pound thrust class and is targeted for 100-passenger aircraft.

8 Things This Runner Is Tired of Hearing

January 14, 2016

If you're a runner, you hear lots of nonsense from non-runners. Am I right? Stuff that makes you want to roll your eyes?

Alison Feller knows what I'm talking about. She recently listed "8 Things Every Runner Is Definitely Tired of Hearing" over on Self.com. It's a fine list, including such reliably annoying things as "Running is bad for your knees" and "How many marathons have you done"?

Still, the list struck us as incomplete. Very incomplete, actually. Here at Dumb Runner we can think of at least eight other things that we are way more tired of hearing.

1. "Who are you? What do you want?"
Relax. I just need to use your bathroom.

2. "Um, your card was declined."
"Um..." if you guys hadn't stopped accepting my personal checks, this wouldn't be a problem. Try it again!

3. "Step out of the vehicle, please."
Give me a break—I'm late to meet some friends for a run. Also, my taxes pay your salary.

4. "I think you've had enough."

I'll tell you when I've had enough! Let me talk to the manager. And *I'll* tell you when I've had enough!

5. "Some penicillin should clear this up."

Let's hope so, Doc. I'm starting to worry my body is building up a resistance.

6. "Sir, some of our other diners are beginning to feel uncomfortable."

How is that my problem? You'd think they've never seen a man's nipples before. Hey, while you're here—could I see the dessert cart?

7. "How did you get past my receptionist?"

Ha ha. Let's just say I "ignored her protestations."

8. "Come on! I can see your junk!"

Oh, do you want to buy me some shorts with a better liner? No? Then shut it!

5 Ways to Make Your Runs More Exciting

January 28, 2016

Guys, are you tired of being bored when you run?

The editors at *Teen Vogue* know exactly how you feel, as usual. They recently published an online article titled "4 Cardio Workouts That Are Way More Exciting than Running." By way of setting the stage, they write:

(L)et's be honest: for many of us running is one of the most boring exercises out there. Whether you're outside in your favorite park or on a treadmill, as soon as your Beyoncé or Taylor Swift playlist ends, you're probably ready to throw in the towel.

I KNOW, RIGHT!

Being bored is literally the worst thing ever! NBB (Never Be Bored)—that is the acronym we live by! That and YOLO!

Except, hold up. Not so fast, *Teen Vogue*. Don't throw in that towel just yet. Running doesn't have to be boring.

We have been running for more than 20 years, including 26 marathons[1] and a whole bunch of other races, and we have discovered plenty of ways to "jazz up" your runs and make them more fun.

Here are five of our favorites, with extra excitement sticks, which is what we call exclamation points, for extra

---

[1] Update: 27 marathons, as of December 2017. But who's counting?

excitement.

1. Run blindfolded!!! Turn your run from "blasé" to "yay!" with a simple piece of cloth tied around your head. Where are you going? What's in front of you? Are the people shouting "Oh my God, look out!" talking to you? Who can say! Ha ha!

Variation: If you don't have a suitable piece of cloth, use a sleep mask or a large bucket.

2. Run with a Roman candle in each hand!!! Carry fireworks and you'll see stars everywhere you run—day and night! Note that a warning label will probably instruct you not to hold the Roman candles in your hands. These warning labels are boring.

Variation: Swap the Roman candles for road flares, or ferrets.

3. Run right down the middle of a four-lane highway!!! Whoa![1] It's hard to be bored with cars, vans, and tractor trailers streaming around you at 70 mph! Pay attention so you don't miss your exit! And remember to run against traffic, for safety!

Variation: For extra excitement, combine this with the blindfold tip.

4. Run while out of your head on crystal meth!!! Forget the "runner's high." This one is instant, and intense! Crystal meth will turn an ordinary 5-miler into a magical rocket-sled ride to the Horsehead Nebula. It also may

---

[1] Again, note the spelling. W-h-o-a. Not *woah*.

induce twitching, angry outbursts, paranoia, dry mouth, and obsessive scratching of your skin. Exciting!

Variation: Try angel dust. PCP.[1]

5. Realize that maybe there is more to life than avoiding boredom at all costs, that a constant need for distraction and instant gratification can and will leave you emotionally and intellectually stunted, that if you fear being alone with your thoughts that much you might benefit from asking yourself why, that perhaps something that seems "boring" can actually be more deeply satisfying than you ever imagined if you're patient enough to push through it, that there could be something incredible awaiting you on the other side, something that could make you a better, healthier, happier human being!!! Variation: Or, you know, just make a longer playlist.

Good luck, readers. Stay excited!

---

[1] In the digital version, this line links to a clip from the 1983 film *Trading Places*. Which I thought was a nice touch.

Also by Mark Remy

The Runner's Rule Book (2009)

The Runner's Field Manual (2010)

C is for Chafing (2011)

The Dumb Runner Training Journal (2015)

Runners of North America (2016)

ABOUT THE AUTHOR

Mark Remy has written four books about running (plus a training journal) and is a columnist for *Runner's World* magazine. As executive editor of RunnersWorld.com, he led the website to a 2008 National Magazine Award for General Excellence Online, its first.

Mark's work has appeared in outlets including NewYorker.com, *Men's Health*, *Bicycling*, *mental_floss*, *Cosmopolitan*, *TV Guide*, and Time Inc. In 2015 he founded DumbRunner.com—"an online destination for runners who enjoy laughter and pie."

A runner for more than 20 years, Mark has finished 27 marathons, including eight Bostons. He lives in Portland, Oregon, with his wife and two children.

For more information, visit markremy.com.

PHOTO CREDITS

Cover illustration: istockphoto.com
Page 16, Child with gun illustration: istockphoto.com
Page 27, Kitten in marathon photo illustration: istockphoto.com
Page 46, Orangutan: istockphoto.com
Page 47, Old woman with camera: Tiago Muraro/Unsplash.com
Page 49, Copernicus magazine cover photo illustration: Wikimedia
Page 53, Justin Trudeau sweatshirt: Shelfies.com
Page 57, Worried woman: istockphoto.com
Page 63, Cute couple: istockphoto.com
Page 67, Run Cleanish photo illustration: istockphoto.com
Page 77, Dog: Caleb Fisher/Unsplash.com
Page 85, Woman on yoga mat: istockphoto.com
Page 92, Laughable finish line: istockphoto.com
Pages 94–98, Stretching illustrations: istockphoto.com
Page 99, Woman at restaurant: istockphoto.com
Page 104, Man on couch: istockphoto.com
Page 108, Woodland lawyer photo illustration: istockphoto.com, Unsplash.com
Page 113, Besty McWesty photo illustration: Unsplash.com
Page 116, Man who carries: istockphoto.com
Page 141, Jerry Orbach photo illustration: istockphoto.com
Page 145, Bike lane: istockphoto.com
Page 155, Mansplaining guy: istockphoto.com
Page 167, Man screaming at child: istockphoto.com
Page 179, Toxin drawing: Mark Remy
Page 185, Muffins: istockphoto.com
Page 200, Socks: Mark Remy
Page 219, Author photo: Jason DeSomer

Made in the USA
Middletown, DE
23 March 2018